CW01647894

Super Simple SEO

by Chris Singleton

A Style Factory book

Style Factory Communications Ltd, Kemp House, 152 City Road, London EC1V 2NX

First published by Style Factory Communications Ltd 2018
Limited company, registered in England no. 10232963

ISBN 978-1-64255-132-7

For my family

Table of contents

1 Three simple rules to remember

It's not uncommon for people to feel a sense of trepidation when they hear the phrase 'search engine optimization.' It immediately conjures up a world of Google trade secrets, complex algorithms and expensive consultants.

It's important not to feel overwhelmed by all this, however, because in essence optimizing a site for Google boils down to three fairly simple rules:

1 Find out what people are searching for in your business area

2 Create really good content about this topic

3 Get links from quality sites to that content

The aim of this book is to help you adhere to these rules, and in the most effective way possible.

It's written for readers who are largely new to the world of search engine optimization (SEO) and want to get an easy-to-understand explanation of the key concepts involved, alongside some actionable steps that can provide some significant improvements to their site's position in search.

Yes, there are some technical steps you'll need to take to optimize your content, and tactics you'll need to use to build links – and we'll cover these in depth in the chapters that follow.

(At the end of the book you'll also find 'cheat sheets' which provide easy-to-follow checklists of key SEO tasks that you'll need to tick off).

But if you always keep the above three 'golden rules' at the heart of all your efforts, you will find that getting Google's algorithms to take your site seriously is a much less challenging proposition than you think.

Let's begin by discussing what an algorithm actually is.

2 What's an algorithm?

Put simply, an algorithm is a list of rules to follow in order to solve a problem.

The problem that a search engine has to solve is how to deliver the best answer to a query from a user; to establish which web page – out of billions of web pages – to display in response to a particular search.

As you might expect, this is a difficult task – and in order to complete it, Google makes use of a series of sophisticated algorithms (in the form of computer programs) which look at your query from a variety of angles.

These algorithms analyse hundreds of different factors to return a list of web pages which are most likely to address a user's query satisfactorily.

How Google's algorithms deal with your query

Once you've entered a search phrase into Google, its algorithms will carry out a series of tasks to try to deliver the best result for you.[1]

These typically involve:

---

[1] https://www.google.com/search/howsearchworks/algorithms/

- Examining what your query really 'means' – for example, when you use the word 'bark' in a search query, a Google algorithm will look at the context you are using it in to try to establish whether you are looking for something to do with dogs or trees.

- Identifying the pages containing keywords which match your query.

- Assessing the quality of the pages containing keywords that match your query – with quality being determined based on things like how recently the content was created; how many people link to the site; and the user experience of the page (these are all 'ranking signals', which we discuss below).

The 'PageRank' algorithm

The first algorithm used by Google to deliver search results was called PageRank.[2]

Developed in 1996 by Google co-founders Larry Page and Sergey Brin (and named after Larry Page), it was designed to measure the importance of web pages based on how many links point to them.

---

[2] https://en.wikipedia.org/wiki/PageRank

According to Google,

> PageRank works by counting the number and quality of links to a page to determine a rough estimate of how important the website is. The underlying assumption is that more important websites are likely to receive more links from other websites.[3]

In the early days of Google, PageRank meant that if you could create a lot of links to your content from other sites, you were likely to receive a good search placement for that content.

The upshot was that the algorithm could be fooled – website owners could 'game' the system by buying links on hundreds of low-quality sites or using link-swapping schemes to help their content rank highly.

So, in subsequent years, Google rolled out a series of updates to PageRank – and indeed introduced entirely new algorithms – to overcome this problem.

---

3 https://tinyurl.com/ybcfnaxg (links to archived 'Facts about Google and Competition' article)

Algorithm updates

Google's algorithms are not static in nature – they are pieces of code that are regularly updated and improved (either by their programmers or increasingly, thanks to machine learning, by the algorithms themselves).[4]

All this is done with a view to improving the quality of search results for users and prevent website owners from using 'black hat' SEO tactics to game the results.[5]

Periodically, SEO experts – based on analysis of website traffic data – identify significant updates to Google's algorithms, or the introduction of new ones. Much like tropical storms, these are often given names by Google and/or the SEO community (you may have heard of algorithm updates called 'Hummingbird,' 'Fred' or 'Pigeon').[6]

It's worth noting that the word 'update' can be a bit misleading: the SEO community often uses it to refer to either a refreshed algorithm or an entirely new one.

---

4 https://searchengineland.com/google-uses-machine-learning-search-algorithms-261158

5 https://www.webopedia.com/TERM/B/Black_Hat_SEO.html

6 https://searchenginewatch.com/sew/opinion/2163436/google-names-algorithm-updates-products

Either way, these 'updates' tend to elevate the importance of certain factors that determine what result should be displayed.

For example, 2015's 'Mobile' update rewarded websites that provided mobile-friendly pages over sites that didn't.
2014's 'Pigeon' update aimed to provide more accurate local search results, rewarding site owners who had created web content focussed on the geographical areas they were operating in.

You can view a list of significant Google algorithm updates on the Search Engine Land website.[7]

Panda and Penguin

Of all the algorithm updates in recent years, two tend to be viewed by SEO experts as being of particular significance:

- 'Panda' (first seen in February 2011)[8]
- 'Penguin' (first seen in April 2012).[9]

(Various improvements and refinements to these continue to be made.)

---

7 https://searchengineland.com/library/google/google-algorithm-updates

8 https://moz.com/learn/seo/google-panda

9 https://moz.com/learn/seo/google-penguin

‘Panda’ gives preferential treatment in search results to websites that contain **high-quality content** over those featuring ‘thin’, ad-heavy or spammy content.

‘Penguin’ gives preferential treatment in search results to websites that are **linked to from high-quality, authoritative websites** over sites that lack these links, or are linked to from low-quality websites.

Alongside PageRank, these two algorithms help inform two of the three golden rules of SEO that I highlighted at the start of this book: *create quality content on your website, and get quality links to it.*

It’s important to remember however, that although these rules are extremely important, they represent a simplified view of SEO – and to ensure successful optimization of a website, there are lots of individual ‘ranking signals’ that you need to take into account.

Ranking signals

Your website’s position in Google search results depends on numerous ‘ranking signals’ – aspects of your site that tell Google’s algorithms that it is worthy of being ranked highly in search.

No SEO expert can claim to know what all of these signals are, as the full technical details of Google’s algorithms are not made publicly available; but it is possible, based on

- patents that Google register
- guidance that Google provides
- first-hand experience of SEO
- industry studies

to make some educated guesses regarding them.

As I've indicated above, ranking signals can include the presence of high quality content on a site and a lot of high quality links pointing to it; but – to give just few examples – they can also include factors such as

- how well a site performs on a mobile device
- how fast it loads
- the structure of a web page's URL
- the conventions used when labelling images.

As you progress through this book, you're going to learn more about the key ranking signals that Google's algorithms are looking for, and find out how you can ensure they are present on your website.

But before you worry about ranking signals, you need to do some keyword research.

Chapter summary

- An algorithm is a list of rules which solves a problem.

- Search engines employ complex algorithms – in the form of computer programs – to deliver search results.

- Google uses several different algorithms, which are periodically updated and often given names.

- The first Google algorithm was PageRank, which is still in use today. This rewards sites that have a lot of backlinks pointing to them.

- Two algorithm updates are worth paying particular attention to: 'Panda' and 'Penguin.' Along with 'PageRank', they indicate that Google significantly rewards sites that (1) contain high quality content and (2) are linked to from high quality websites.

- Google's algorithms look for the presence of multiple 'ranking signals' on your website to determine its placement in search results.

- A wide range of ranking signals need to be associated with your site – for example, it needs to load fast; contain relevant right keywords; have quality links pointing to it.

The key ranking signals will be outlined and discussed in depth throughout the remainder of this book.

3 Keyword research

You can optimize your site for any words or phrases you like – and write suitably fantastic content for them – but if you choose the wrong ones, you can end up with very little traffic.

That's why keyword research is so important, and it's the first thing you should do when optimizing your site for search engines.

What's a keyword?

As you might expect, a keyword is a phrase you'd like your site to 'rank for' in search results – i.e., so that if somebody types it into Google, your site appears in the top set of results.

A keyword can contain one word – for example 'camera' – or it can contain several (i.e., 'what is the best type of DSLR camera?').

SEO experts usually divide keywords up into three main categories, based on how long a keyword is:

- **Head** – a one-word keyword (i.e., 'car')
- **Body** – a two to three-word keyword ('buy car')
- **Tail** – a long, rather specific phrase or question ('where can I buy a VW car in North London?')

Head keywords can generate a lot of searches and drive huge quantities of traffic to a site, but they are usually extremely hard to rank for.

In many cases, head keywords don't lead to a high proportion of sales either, because they can be a bit vague in nature.

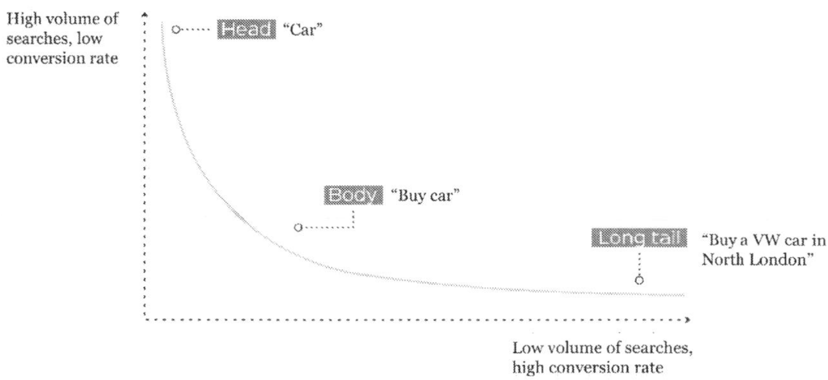

This graph shows the relationship between head, body and tail keywords – and conversion rates.

In the 'head' example above, the person searching for 'car' could have been looking for a wide range of car-related products or services – a new car, car insurance, car repair and so on; it's unlikely that the results presented would have adequately met his/her needs, and would probably not have led to an immediate sale (or 'conversion').

Body and tail keywords don't drive as much traffic to sites as head term keywords, but because the search term is much more specific, the traffic they *do* attract is from people who are much more likely to be interested in the products or services featured in search results. This makes a sale more likely.

For example, a 'tail' query for 'Buy a VW car in North London' will generate some very relevant results for the person making that search, and might very well lead to some quick business for the dealer who is fortunate enough to top the search results for that query.

So, most keyword research focuses on trying to identify body and tail keywords that can realistically drive traffic and conversions.

So how do you perform keyword research?

Keyword research involves finding out three key pieces of information:

1) the keywords that people are using to search for products / services in your market

2) the volume of searches for each of those keywords

3) how difficult it will be to rank for each keyword (this is based on how many existing authoritative sites or pages already perform well in search results for those keywords).

When you have these three pieces of information, you can usually identify the phrase (or phrases) that your site should be optimized for.

This is because you have enough data to find a 'sweet spot' – keywords that are popular enough to generate a decent amount of traffic, without being *so* popular that there are already lots of other sites dominating search results for these terms.

Let's illustrate the point with an example. Suppose you are a manufacturer of dark blue guitars and you're setting up a new website to sell your wares. In your music-loving locality there might be

- 20,000 monthly searches for 'guitars'
- 10,000 for 'navy guitars'
- 5,000 for 'dark blue guitars'
- 3,000 for 'indigo guitars'
- 1,000 'midnight blue guitars.'

There might also be

- 50 websites providing an exact match in search results for 'guitars'
- 10 for 'navy guitars'
- 8 for 'dark blue guitars'

- 2 for 'indigo guitars'
- 1 for 'midnight blue guitars.'

The above knowledge is power. It allows you to optimize your new guitar-selling website in a way that will strike a balance between the volume of searches for a particular phrase, and the existing competition for that phrase.

Based on the above (imaginary!) data, I'd probably be tempted to focus on 'indigo guitars' as the phrase I would optimize my site around: it generates enough searches per month to make it worthwhile focusing on as a keyword, without there being too many sites offering exact match results for it.

But how do you get your hands on these kinds of statistics? It usually involves keyword research tools.

Using keyword research tools

Keyword research tools let you check how many people are searching for a particular keyword and get a list of suggestions of similar phrases. Some well-known ones include:

- Ahrefs[10]

---

[10] https://ahrefs.com/

- Moz Pro[11]
- SE Cockpit[12]
- SEMRush[13]
- Serpstat[14]

These are all paid-for tools, and their monthly costs can be quite high depending on how much of their functionality you require and how many SEO projects you want to use them for.

(Another more basic option is to use Google's Keyword Planner, but you can only use this if you are an active Google Ads customer).[15]

What can keyword research tools tell you?

When you enter a phrase into a keyword research tool, you'll typically see three things:

- The **number of searches** being made each month for that phrase.

- A list of **keyword suggestions** based on the phrase you entered and the number of searches for each.

---

11 https://moz.com/products/pro

12 https://secockpit.com/

13 https://www.semrush.com/

14 https://serpstat.com/

15 https://adwords.google.com/intl/en_us/home/tools/keyword-planner/

- The **'keyword' difficulty score** – how hard the tool thinks it will be for you to rank for your chosen keyword (and the other suggestions provided). This is based on how many high-quality sites/pages are already ranking for the keywords involved.

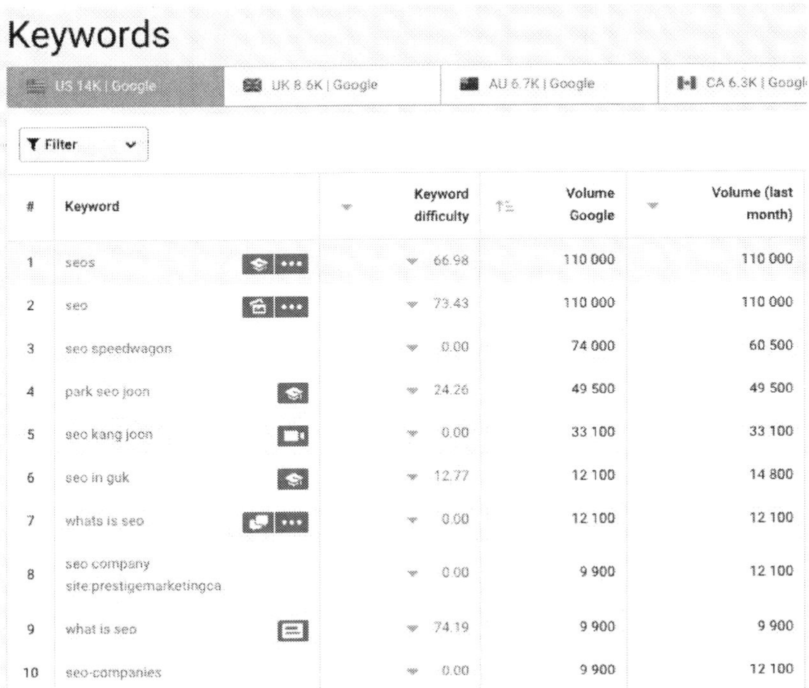

Keywords

US 14K | Google · UK 8.6K | Google · AU 6.7K | Google · CA 6.3K | Googl

Filter

#	Keyword	Keyword difficulty	Volume Google	Volume (last month)
1	seos	66.98	110 000	110 000
2	seo	73.43	110 000	110 000
3	seo speedwagon	0.00	74 000	60 500
4	park seo joon	24.26	49 500	49 500
5	seo kang joon	0.00	33 100	33 100
6	seo in guk	12.77	12 100	14 800
7	whats is seo	0.00	12 100	12 100
8	seo company site:prestigemarketingca	0.00	9 900	12 100
9	what is seo	74.19	9 900	9 900
10	seo-companies	0.00	9 900	12 100

Using Serpstat as a keyword research tool lets you see how many searches there are per month for a particular search phrase, alongside the 'keyword difficulty' indicator (the latter tells you how hard it will be to rank for a particular phrase, with higher values indicating increased difficulty).

Some tools, such as Ahrefs, also give you an estimate of how many 'backlinks' — links from other sites to your content — you will need to generate in order to rank on the first page of search results. (I explain backlinks in more depth in Chapter 7 — but for now it's enough to know that generally speaking, the more backlinks that point to a piece of content, the better it performs in search).

The trick is to use all this information to strike a balance between the number of searches being made for a particular keyword, and its keyword difficulty.

You'll need to zoom in on keywords that generate a reasonably large number of searches whilst simultaneously having a low keyword difficulty score.

However, you must also remember that your keyword needs to be very relevant to the service you're providing on your site too. If, for example, you *rent* electric guitars, a keyword such as 'how to *make* an electric guitar' – even if you knew it could generate a lot of visitors to your site – might not be terribly useful.

Seeing what your competitors are up to

Another useful thing that many keyword research tools do is show you a list of keywords that are prevalent on your competitors' sites.

If you enter a competitor's URL into a keyword research tool, you'll usually have the option to view all the keywords that are driving organic traffic to their site.

This may spark some keyword ideas for you, or, if you're feeling ambitious, prompt you to compete for some of the same keywords.

Casting the net wider

Whilst keyword research tools are undoubtedly helpful in identifying keywords, there are a couple of problems in relying on them *exclusively* for suggestions.

The first problem is that a lot of people use them, so any keyword suggestions they provide are potentially being seen by your competitors too (this means that a lot of businesses end up zooming in on the same keywords, and chasing the same search results).

The second is that suggestions provided by keyword research tools are often a bit *too* closely related to a keyword you put in.

For example, if you enter a keyword like 'car repairs' into a keyword research tool, you'll often end up with a lot of suggestions like 'auto repair', 'car repair estimates', 'car repair shop' and so on – but you might not see more niche phrases such as 'exhaust repairs', 'dent removal' or 'car repair in Newtown.'

This is a problem because the latter set of keywords might actually be more relevant to your business, easier to rank for and ultimately more lucrative.

Thankfully there are quite a few ways that you compile a more exhaustive list of relevant, long-tail keywords – SEO expert Brian Dean has some excellent tips in this regard:[16]

- **Brainstorm**: use your intuition, experience and knowledge of your market locally to draw up a list of keywords that you think are related to your business area. And then sense-check them using a keyword research tool.

- **Look in forums** that are related to your business area for threads containing potentially relevant keywords.

- **Search on Wikipedia** for a subject related to your business, then look at the table of contents of the article – it will often contain a list of related keywords which you might have overlooked.

- **Search for a topic on Reddit** and look at the discussion titles – they'll often contain potentially useful keywords.

---

[16] https://backlinko.com/keyword-research

Contents [hide]

- 1 History
  - 1.1 1957–1962: Formation, Hamburg, and UK popularity
  - 1.2 1963–1966: Beatlemania and touring years
    - 1.2.1 *Please Please Me* and *With the Beatles*
    - 1.2.2 "British Invasion"
    - 1.2.3 *A Hard Day's Night*
    - 1.2.4 *Beatles for Sale*, *Help!* and *Rubber Soul*
    - 1.2.5 Controversy, final tour and *Revolver*
  - 1.3 1966–1970: Studio years and break-up
    - 1.3.1 *Sgt. Pepper's Lonely Hearts Club Band*
    - 1.3.2 *Magical Mystery Tour*, the White Album and *Yellow Submarine*
    - 1.3.3 *Abbey Road*, *Let It Be* and break-up
  - 1.4 1970–present: After the break-up
    - 1.4.1 1970s
    - 1.4.2 1980s
    - 1.4.3 1990s
    - 1.4.4 2000s
    - 1.4.5 2010s
- 2 Musical style and development
  - 2.1 Influences
  - 2.2 Genres
  - 2.3 Contribution of George Martin
  - 2.4 In the studio
- 3 Legacy
- 4 Awards and achievements
- 5 Members
- 6 Discography
- 7 Song catalogue
- 8 Notes
- 9 Citations
- 10 Sources
- 11 Further reading
- 12 External links

Wikipedia can give you some interesting ideas for keywords. In the above example, this table of contents is displayed as part of the entry for 'The Beatles.' Using this could generate some useful keyword ideas which you might not otherwise not have considered – for example 'Hamburg', 'British Invasion' or 'George Martin.'

Identifying the keywords to optimize your site for

By the end of all this you should have a sizeable list of keywords which are relevant to your business. The trick is now to work out which ones you should optimize your site for, by finding the 'sweet spot' mentioned earlier.

This should be now a fairly straightforward task: you need to enter your final list of keywords back into your keyword research tool, and look at the search volumes and keyword difficulty scores.

The keywords which combine a good search volume with a low difficulty score (and, where available, a low 'estimated backlinks to rank' figure) are the ones you should be treating as the focus keywords for your site.

Once you've got your keyword(s) ready to go, it's time to start looking at creating some great content for them.

Chapter summary

- Keyword research involves identifying keywords that generate a reasonably large number of searches, but which don't feature heavily in search results.

- 'Tail keywords' – longer search phrases containing a fair amount of detail – tend to be more lucrative than one-word 'head' keywords, and are often easier to rank for.

- To identify suitable focus keywords for your project, you will need to use a keyword research tool.

- Brainstorming and researching what words people use when talking about your business on forums and discussion sites can also be helpful in identifying potentially lucrative keywords.

- Once you've shortlisted some keywords, use your keyword research tool to check the volume of searches for and 'keyword difficulty' of each. The keywords which combine a reasonable number of searches with a low keyword difficulty score are the ones you should optimize your content for.

4 Creating quality content

OK, so you've carried out some detailed keyword research, and you're confident you've now got some keywords that could, when tied to a piece of great content, perform really well for you.

But how do you actually come up with that great content? Well, before you start writing or publishing anything, it's a good idea to consider what format is going to deliver the best results in search.

Which format is best?

There is a myriad of ways to present a piece of content online – you can publish some text on a static page; upload a video to Youtube; post something on Facebook; share an image on Pinterest; write a blog post...

If attracting visitors via a search engine to your site is the primary goal, I would argue that focusing on writing blog posts, which you publish on your own domain, is nearly always the best option (at least when starting out in SEO).

There are a few reasons for this:

- With blog posts, you have the scope to explore a topic in considerable depth and at considerable length. This is not really the case with static web pages, which tend to be more about providing a short and simple overview of a product or service. (And as I shall show later, long pages tend to perform better in search results.)

- The features you'll usually find on blog posts – commenting and sharing options – can be used to generate important ranking signals.

- The text on a blog post which you publish on your own domain is easily indexed by search engines – this is not the case with some sites or formats (for cxample, it's often quite hard for search engines to index Facebook posts owing to the network's privacy settings; and videos, owing to their non-text-based format, are sometimes harder to index / categorize accurately).

- Although there are benefits to having pieces of content which rank well on third party sites (like Youtube or Pinterest), it's more beneficial to you as a site owner if any external links to a good piece of content point back to *your* website instead of one belonging to a third party.

All that said, it depends entirely on the piece of content.

If you are a filmmaker, for example, or if your business model is based on creating how-to-videos, you are obviously going to need to use a service like Youtube to present your content (you'll find some Youtube SEO tips on the Search Engine Watch website).[17]

Similarly, musicians are going to benefit from using platforms like Soundcloud to host their content.

But generally speaking, when it comes to content production, my advice would be to focus on blog posts as the main format in which to present content (and of course you can always embed video and audio, which you host on other platforms in these posts anyway).

How to create a great blog post

Ensure you have a great writer

It sounds obvious, but it's worth saying: if you want to publish great blog content, the first thing you need is a great writer.

In this world of DIY marketing and publishing, it's tempting to dive straight in and produce your own posts; but before you do that it's worth considering if you're the right person to write the content for your site.

To create a strong blog post, you need to have:

---

[17] https://searchenginewatch.com/sew/how-to/2340726/5-advanced-youtube-seo-tactics-to-drive-more-traffic-to-your-videos-website

- a clear understanding of your business area and the niche topics that you will be writing about
- a clear understanding of the audience that will be reading the post
- perfect spelling and grammar
- a personality that shines through in the posts.

If that doesn't sound like you, it might be time either spend some time working on meeting the above criteria before you start blogging, or to hire somebody who already does.

Focus on solving problems and delivering value

It's all very well talking about creating 'great' or 'quality' content but people have very different ideas of what's great; it's a very subjective term.

And 'great' does not guarantee 'visible', either. Millions of amazing articles, videos and songs that could easily be described as great or even potentially life-changing live on the internet – but never surface on search engines.

And that's because – rightly or wrongly – Google's search algorithms usually focus on meeting immediate needs rather than suggesting enjoyable or meaningful content.

This is because people searching for something on Google usually have a *problem*. They want to know how to make an apple-crumble. Or what the safest car is. Or which piece of software is best for doing their accounts. Or where they can listen to the latest U2 album. (As discussed in the previous chapter, you will have identified the relevant problem for *your* potential customers by doing your keyword research).

Your job as a content creator is to provide a great solution to your readers' problem – and in the clearest, most informative way possible. As such, every aspect of your content – title, introductory paragraph, images and conclusions – should focus relentlessly on this. Forget sales pitches or waffle about how great your company is – focus on delivering real value to the reader. Because if your reader perceives your content as being valuable, they are likely to...

- stay longer on your page
- share your post on social media
- create a link to it on their site.

All of these actions, as we will discover later in the book, can ultimately have a very beneficial impact on your search results.

Be original

Never 'scrape' content from other sources – Google's algorithms are wise to that and you won't reap any SEO benefits from republishing or reformatting existing content from others on your site.[18]

Additionally, in an age of 'churnalism,' readers can switch off quickly if they are confronted with material that they've encountered before.

So be original – do your own research where possible and put your own spin on things.

Create an engaging post title

It's vital to get the title of your post right.

First, it gives you a clear direction on what you're meant to be writing about and something you can use to evaluate the final contents of your post. If your article's content doesn't do justice to its title, or answer the question posed by it, it's time to go back to the drawing board.

Second, the title of a post is its most visible aspect in Google search results, and the only clickable part of a result. Titles are scanned very quickly by Google users and your post will only ever by clicked on if its title comes across as highly relevant to the query they've just entered.

---

18 https://support.google.com/webmasters/answer/2721312?hl=en

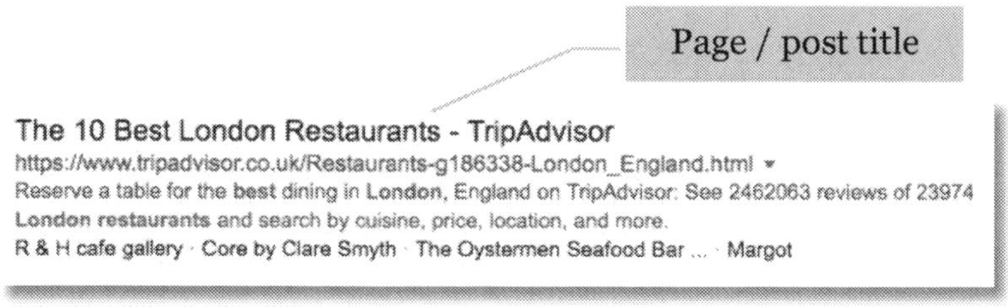

The above search result is returned as the number one result for a search for 'best places to eat in London'. Note how relevant the title is to the query.

These users' clicks determine a 'clickthrough rate' (or 'CTR'). Now, there's currently a debate raging as to whether CTR is a ranking factor.

Many SEO experts insist that it is, and argue that Google assigns more importance over time to posts that have a higher proportion of clickthroughs than others in search.[19]

Others say that CTR is too easily 'gamed' and as such cannot be a ranking factor. As is often the case with SEO, because there are conflicting studies and we don't have access to Google's algorithms, we just don't know.

Either way, it makes sense to make your post titles as engaging as possible. A good title with a high CTR means that your post is more likely to be read in the first place and subsequently shared and

[19] https://moz.com/blog/does-organic-ctr-impact-seo-rankings-new-data

linked to: both actions are very important for long-term success in search rankings.

And if Google *is* using CTR as a ranking signal, you'll get some SEO juice out of a title with a good CTR too.

Here are some tactics you might want to employ to create a title that generates clickthroughs:

- **Use 'how to' and listicle titles to draw people in.** 'How to' posts make it obvious that they're providing a solution to something – and as discussed above, it's solutions that people are usually looking for when they use a search engine. Listicle titles ('5 ways to improve your sex life' etc.) have a good track record of encouraging clickthroughs, because they promise 'good value' for a user's click – i.e., one clickthrough to your wonderful post will provide 5 ways to have a better time in bed.

- **Don't be vague**: ensure your titles spell out the solutions your posts contain. For example, a title of 'How to tie a shoelace' is preferable to 'Shoelace tips' – the former makes it clear that your post is about tying shoelaces, while the latter leaves the reader guessing about what sort of shoelace-related advice they're going to receive in your post.

- **Don't give *everything* away in the title**. If for example, you're writing an article comparing two products, don't immediately let your readers know which is best – a title of 'Apples vs Oranges – which fruit is the best for you?' would generally generate more clickthroughs than 'Apples vs Oranges – Oranges are definitely better for you.'

- **Be punchy and avoid waffle**. As we'll discover later on in this book, there is an argument for using relatively long titles (because they contain more 'long-tail' keywords which increase the chances of your post being discovered in search). However, it's important to strike the right balance here: long, incomprehensible, meandering titles will not win you any readers.

Write a killer opening paragraph

Once somebody has clicked through to your post, you want to keep them there for as long as possible. The longer somebody stays on your post, the greater the 'dwell time' will be – and dwell time is considered by many SEO experts to be a ranking signal (not least because Google have patented the idea of a longer stay on a page denoting a more relevant result).[20]

---

[20] https://tinyurl.com/y53wf2v9 (links to Google patent on dwell time).

The first paragraph of your article is your best chance, then, of keeping a reader on a page long enough to read it in depth.

This means – and again, going back to our 'problem solving' approach – that your job in the first paragraph is to outline your reader's problem and show how, over the course of your article, you're going to solve it.

Use long-form content

'Long-form content' – long articles which cover topics in great detail – is generally agreed by SEO experts to perform better in Google than short articles.

Not only have studies indicated that this is likely to be the case,[21] but Google has dropped some pretty big hints to this effect too.[22]

There are a few reasons why long-form articles may perform better in search results than shorter ones:

- Due to their length, they naturally contain more long tail keywords – and as such are more likely to pop up in search results.

---

[21] https://neilpatel.com/blog/why-you-need-to-create-evergreen-long-form-content-and-how-to-produce-it/

[22] https://webmasters.googleblog.com/2013/08/in-depth-articles-in-search-results.html

- They provide a valuable, comprehensive resource that people want to link to from their own websites and blogs.

- Because they're longer, people spend more time reading them – thus increasing 'dwell time' (which as discussed above, may be a ranking signal).

- If Google's comments on in-depth articles are to be believed, its algorithms are designed to reward them.[23]

Given the above, it makes sense – in most contexts – to focus on publishing long, in-depth blog posts rather than short ones. If I had to choose between publishing one comprehensive 2000-word post a month or one 300-word post a week, I would definitely opt for the former approach: in my experience, quality tends to beat frequency when it comes to SEO.

However, it's important not to focus on the 'long' aspect over the 'in-depth' side of things. It's quite easy to write a very long-winded blog post; much harder to ensure that it engages throughout and ends up being genuinely useful to the reader.

Here are a few tips that will help you create informative, valuable long-form content:

---

[23] https://webmasters.googleblog.com/2013/08/in-depth-articles-in-search-results.html

- Ensure you are creating content that people are actually searching for and want to read – as discussed earlier, keyword research is your friend here.

- Plan your post well: sketch out your article in advance, breaking it down into easy-to-understand sub-topics.

- Use interesting images and videos where necessary (and relevant) to enhance your post.

- Assume your readers are not experts in whatever it is you're writing about (if they were, they probably wouldn't need to Google it!). Avoid being over technical – explaining things clearly, patiently and fully throughout your post.

- Avoid waffle; ensure that each section of your post provides easy-to-understand and relevant information.

- Provide outbound links, where appropriate, to related resources. Yes, this can take users off your site – but it lets them know that you have researched your topic in depth, and some studies show that outbound links can also provide an SEO benefit too.[24]

---

[24] https://www.rebootonline.com/blog/long-term-outgoing-link-experiment/

Make your content very readable

Ensure that your content is easy to read. This means:

- using simple, clear typefaces – opinions vary on the best ones to use but the general consensus is that sans-serif fonts work best on screen

- breaking up your content where appropriate with sub-headings and bullet-points – this allows people to scan your articles easily and locate the parts that are most relevant to them

- using short sentences and paragraphs where possible – again, this aids the 'scannability' and readability of your content.

Update your blog posts

You might think that once you've written your in-depth, informative blog post that it's job done.

Well actually, no. A Google patent about information retrieval based on historical data indicates that posts that are updated periodically may be given more weight in search results than posts that always remain static.[25]

So when appropriate, update your posts so that they contain new research, supporting material and so on. Not only will this potentially send a positive ranking signal to Google, but it makes your content better (and more accurate) over time.

Once you've got your content ready, it's time to fine-tune it so that it stands every chance of ranking well in search.

This is where on-page SEO comes in.

Chapter summary

- Choosing the best format for your content is important. This will vary by business and project type but in most cases, blog posts generate the most 'indexable' content and provide the easiest way to generate content that performs well in search.

- Ensure that the person writing your posts has an extensive knowledge of your business area along with good writing

---

25 http://patft.uspto.gov/netacgi/nph-Parser?Sect1=PTO2&Sect2=HITOFF&p=1&u=%2Fnetahtml%2FPTO%2Fsearch-adv.htm&r=1&f=G&l=50&d=PALL&S1=07346839&OS=PN/07346839&RS=PN/07346839

skills.

- Write articles that solve problems, and accurately address known search queries. You can do this by using 'how to' posts and listicles to provide 'actionable' content.

- Be original – never scrape or duplicate content.

- Ensure that your content's title is as engaging and as relevant to key search queries as possible.

- Focus in particular on creating great opening paragraphs that make it clear how you are going to solve the reader's key problem. These keep the reader on the page longer, which may improve a page's position in search results.

- Use long-form content – write in-depth articles that have a high word- count, contain supporting images and videos and provide outbound links to quality reference material.

- Ensure that your content is easy to read on screen by making use of sans-serif typefaces.

- Make your content easy for readers to scan by using sub-headings, short paragraphs and bullet points.

5 On-page SEO

On-page SEO means laying out your site content in a way that makes it easy for search engines to understand what your pages are about.

I consider on-page SEO to be one of the more straightforward aspects of optimizing your site. It's relatively formulaic, in that there are a series of simple steps you can take to ensure that a page is optimized for a particular keyword.

Below you will find a list of what I believe are the key on-page SEO boxes to tick.

Ensure you use search-friendly URLs for your site pages

Google is quite clear about the fact that its algorithms prefer a simple URL structure.[26]

As such your page URLs should

- be short
- contain your focus keywords.

---

[26] https://support.google.com/webmasters/answer/76329

This means that instead of using a page address such as

www.johnscars.com/resources/carlist/subs_2/p1235.asp?q=5

you should opt for something like

www.johnscars.com/volkswagen-polo

Note the use of a hyphen to separate out 'Volkswagen' and 'Polo' in the URL. This helps search engines identify the keywords more easily, as highlighted by Google itself:

> Consider using punctuation in your URLs. The URL **http://www.example.com/green-dress.html** is much more useful to us than **http://www.example.com/greendress.html**. We recommend that you use hyphens (-) instead of underscores (_) in your URLs.[27]

It's unclear how much Google uses keywords in URLs to categorize content – spammy use of keywords in URLs and domains by site owners in the past is thought to have led to a certain demotion of keywords in URLs as a ranking signal.

---

[27] https://support.google.com/webmasters/answer/76329

However, in my view the above advice from Google on hyphenation implies it still *does* use keywords to understand (and thus – to a degree at least – rank the content).

Even if the Google doesn't use keywords in URLs to categorize content to the extent it once did, inserting them into URLs can still have an important SEO benefit, because the URLs can end up as anchor text.

We'll discuss anchor text in more depth later, but basically it is the clickable words used in a link from one page to another, i.e.,

> Did you know that we offer both WordPress and Squarespace web design services?

Because search engines use anchor text to categorize the content being linked to, they prefer anchor text containing words which help them do just that.

In the above example, 'web design services' has been chosen as the anchor text, forming a backlink that tells Google to index the target page as being about web design.

However, URLs frequently get copied and pasted onto other web pages verbatim, i.e.,

See www.stylefactoryproductions.com/web-design/ for information about Style Factory's web design services.

and in such situations, the URL itself becomes the anchor text.

Now, because the words 'web design' are in the above URL, it has generated anchor text which will still tell Google what your page is about.

(If the URL that had been copied and pasted was *www.stylefactoryproductions.com/wd1234.asp*, it would have been less valuable).

Start your page title with your keywords

Your page title is the text you see at the top of the browser window – and it's also the headline that comes up in search results.

Google attaches a lot of importance to the words used in a page title, so wherever possible your page title should always start with your focus keyword. Not only does this tell Google what your content is primarily about, but it makes it easier for search engine users to spot your content in search results.

Let's say you run a music instrument shop, Jimbob's Music, and you want to set up a page selling vintage blue pianos.

Instead of putting the company name first, you should put the product at the start, followed by the company name – i.e.,

'Vintage Blue Pianos – Jimbob's Music'.

Expand your page title with helpful 'long-tail' keywords

In addition to putting your target keyword near the start of your page title, it's important to add to it keywords - or 'modifiers' – which will increase the chances of your page performing well in 'long-tail' searches (i.e., those where users are combining multiple keywords in their query).

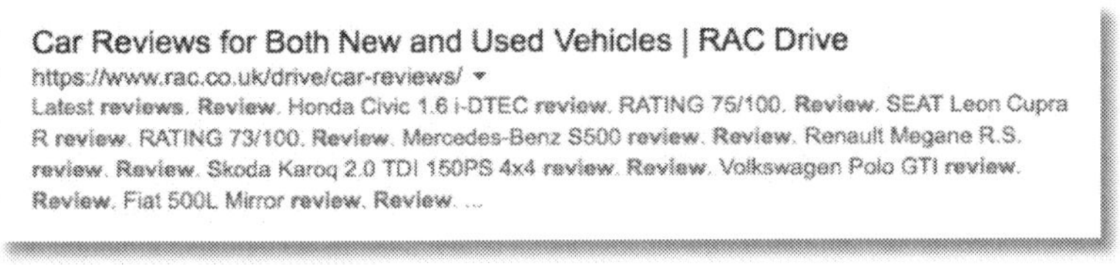

In the above example, 'modifiers' have been added to the page title. This means that the page stands a good chance of ranking not just for its focus keyword of 'car reviews' but for searches such as 'new car reviews', 'used vehicle reviews' and 'RAC car reviews.'.

For example, if you had a page which was reviewing the new Volkswagen Touran, a page title of

Volkswagen Touran

would be less likely to perform well in relevant searches as

Volkswagen Touran Review: Is VW's new 7-seater MPV any good?

The additional keywords cover more bases and will help your page to perform better in a wider range of tail searches (i.e., 'VW MPV review', 'MPV reviews', '7 seater MPV' etc.).

Ensure that your H1 tag contains your target keyword

Your H1 ('heading 1') tag is one of the most important pieces of content on your page and the general consensus amongst SEO experts is that Google attaches great importance to it. Essentially, it's a key way of telling Google what the page is principally about.

Because of this, your H1 should always contain your target keyword.

You can find more information about headings on W3Schools.com's HTML Headings section.[28]

[28] https://www.w3schools.com/html/html_headings.asp

Ensure your page titles and H1 tags are unique

To avoid confusing search engines, or giving them the impression that you've got duplicate content on your site (something that Google is not keen on), you should make sure that all your page titles and H1 tags are unique.[29]

Write a compelling meta description

Your 'meta-description' is a summary of your page content that is often displayed by search engines in search results (under the page title).

It has to be as good as possible – not because Google uses it to index your content, but because good meta-descriptions encourage a higher clickthrough rate (CTR) to your site from search results.

Although there is debate amongst the SEO community as to whether CTR is a ranking factor, it unquestionably gets more people onto your website, which in turns leads to more backlink generation opportunities (with backlinks of course, being vital to improving your search ranking).[30]

---

29 https://support.google.com/webmasters/answer/66359?hl=en

30 https://searchenginewatch.com/2016/09/22/ctr-as-a-ranking-factor-what-we-know-so-far-and-how-to-action-it/

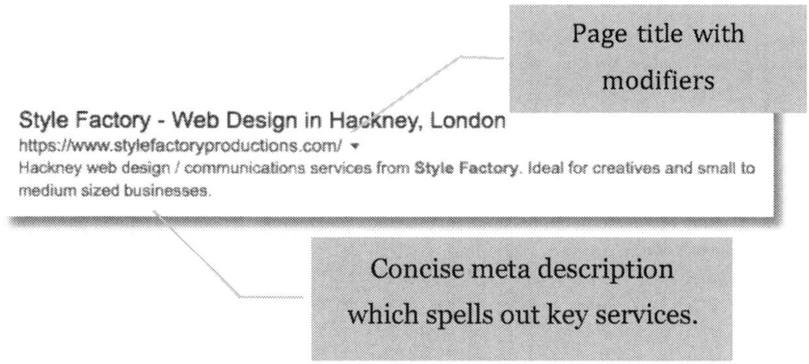

(Another benefit of writing a strong meta-description is that it is often included in the preview link when shared on social media. A good meta- description will drive more clickthroughs here too).

Include your target keyword in the first paragraph of your page content

You should ideally include your target keyword in the first paragraph of your page copy. There are a couple of reasons for this.

First, doing so may help search engines categorize the information better and treat your page preferentially in search results.[31]

Second, if users arrive at your page and see the keyword in the first paragraph, they're more likely to view the content as relevant to

[31] https://yoast.com/text-structure-important-seo/

their search query, and will therefore probably stay longer on the page – thus increasing 'dwell time,' which many SEO experts believe to be a ranking signal (particularly for sites that are attaining first-page search results for competitive keywords).[32]

Include your target keyword in some H2s

It makes sense to include your keyword in one or two of your H2s (heading 2s).

In a similar way to including your keywords in H1s and your first paragraph, this signals to both readers and search engines that your content is answering relevant queries.

Include your target keyword a few times in your body copy

As you might expect, it's a good idea to include your keyword a few times in the body copy of your article.

Don't overdo it – as keyword stuffing can be interpreted negatively by Google – but ensure that your keyword does appear enough times to convince a search engine that your article is genuinely about that keyword.[33]

---

32 https://ahrefs.com/blog/dwell-time/

33 https://support.google.com/webmasters/answer/66358?hl=en

Make sure your content is fairly long

As I outlined in Chapter 4, longer pages tend to rank better in search – so long as they are well written.

To recap the three main reasons for this:

- They contain more keywords, improving performance in 'long tail' searches.

- They keep users on the page longer (thus increasing 'dwell time', a potential ranking signal).

- If your content deals with a topic in depth, it is more likely to engage and encourage people either to create links to or share it online, both of which can improve page ranking over time.

The current consensus is that pages should ideally be longer than 1000 words; however, if you're going to write long pages, ensure that the content is extremely strong.

Poorly-written long pages, deliberately stuffed with keywords, are unlikely to feature in search results – search engines are clever enough to spot spam.

Increase dwell time by including videos, images and infographics on your page

Dwell time – the amount of time that elapses between a user clicking on a search result and returning to search results – is considered by some SEO experts to be a ranking signal, because the longer a user stays on your page before considering other articles presented in search results, the more likely it is that your page is answering their query appropriately.

As this article on ahrefs.com explains, the jury is still apparently out on whether or not dwell time is a ranking factor, but there are quite a few strong arguments as to why it might well be.[34] Accordingly, it is a good idea to supplement your text with videos and other visual content that keep your users on your page longer – so long as any content you add is (1) 100% relevant to your page topic and (2) doesn't add hugely to your page load time (we'll discuss page load time shortly).

Add some LSI keywords to your posts

LSI stands for Latent Semantic Indexing – a mathematical technique used by search engines to identify, on the basis of the

34 https://ahrefs.com/blog/dwell-time/

types of phrases used throughout a text, what your content is about.[35]

You don't need to get bogged down too much in the technicalities of this, but you do need to remember that 'LSI keywords' can help improve on-page SEO.

Simply put, LSI keywords are phrases that contextualize your article. If, for example, you were writing a post about trains, then including words like 'train times', 'carriages' and 'stations' would make it far more likely that search engines would categorize your post as being about a form of public transport rather than the rock band Train.

The takeaway here is that you should sprinkle related keywords throughout any content you create. A lot of the time this means adding synonyms to your page – i.e., instead of exclusively using your target keyword throughout the page, consider replacing it occasionally with a word that means the same thing – 'VW' as well as 'Volkswagen'; 'aeroplane/airplane' as well as 'plane'; 'pub' alongside 'bar' etc.

---

35 https://en.wikipedia.org/wiki/Latent_semantic_analysis#Latent_semantic_indexing

If you're writing quality content, it's likely that you'll do this naturally – but it's always worth reviewing your copy after you've written it to ensure that it contains a healthy sprinkling of LSI keywords.

Optimize your images using alt text

Optimizing your images is an easy way to improve the SEO of your content. This is easily done, through use of 'alternative text' (alt text).

Alt text is an attribute you add to your images via HTML code. It serves three main functions:

- It provides some text that can be read aloud by screen reading software when it encounters an image, so that those with visual disabilities can get a description of it.
- It's displayed in place of an image in browsers if the image file cannot be loaded.
- It tells search engines about the image, and, by extension the page content.

The main function of interest to us here is the third one.

Because search engines use alt text to determine what a page is about, it makes sense where possible to include target keywords in it. However, this should not be done entirely at the expense of accessibility – ideally, your alt text should explain the picture adequately for any visually impaired users AND feature the target keyword.

Another way to optimize images is simply to include your target keyword in the file name. Again, however, I'd refrain from overdoing this. If writing a post which is primarily about dog food, I'd use a filename of dog-food.jpg on a picture of a tin of dog food – but not on a picture of a dog-collar.

The trick with image optimization – and indeed all types of search engine optimization – is to avoid techniques which can easily be spotted as being obviously spammy by search engines.

Use outbound links in your content

Studies have shown that outbound links – links to sites other than your own – within a piece of content can help search engines figure out the context of your page and have positive effects on SEO.[36]

Linking to relevant and authoritative sites can be particularly beneficial.

---

[36] https://www.searchenginejournal.com/study-shows-outgoing-links-have-positive-effects-on-seo/157431/

Create internal links

It's a good idea to create internal links within your site, mainly from high authority pages (ones that are already doing well in search) to lower authority ones that you want to rank for. This can pass on a bit of 'link juice' and help raise visibility in search results.

Remember however that the links need to be relevant; i.e., on a page about cat food don't link to a page about cars unless there is an extremely good reason to do so!

Encourage social sharing

It's really important to place social sharing buttons prominently on every page on your site. Although Google says that social shares of your content don't influence your site ranking,[37] they do generate more visitors to your site – and the more visitors you get, the greater the chances are of people creating backlinks to your site (and getting backlinks, as we shall discover, is an absolutely crucial part of getting visible in search results).

---

37 https://www.youtube.com/watch?v=udqtSM-6QbQ

You can use tools like Addthis and Sharethis to add social sharing buttons to your site.[38] These tools also allow you to track and analyse shares of your content.

Encourage commenting on your posts

There is a bit of a debate on this one, but my view is that encouraging people to post comments on your blog is a good thing to do from an SEO perspective.

First, they generate a lot of content on a page, and increase the number of LSI keywords on your page. I've often found comments appearing in search results, indicating that search engines both index and value them.

Second, they indicate that people are interested in your content and that there is an active community on your site. There have been noises from Google in the past that this is a good thing.[39]

By 'encouraging commenting' I mean being quite proactive about it – i.e., including visible calls to action within blog posts to add a comment.

---

[38] See http://www.addthis.com/ and https://www.sharethis.com/ for Addthis and Sharethis respectively. Note that these services may sell some of your analytics data to advertisers.

[39] http://www.thesempost.com/comments-good-for-google-seo/

One thing I would definitely suggest you do however if you facilitate and encourage commenting on your posts is ensure that all comments are moderated.

Low-quality, spammy comments should be deleted as Google is likely to view them as a negative signal; only genuinely useful comments and enquiries should remain on your blog posts.

Encourage people to create links to your content

As we shall discover later in the book, backlinks (links to your site from others) are absolutely vital to achieving a good placement in search results. Accordingly, it makes sense to place encouragements to your readers to create links to your content within the content itself.

Even if only a small proportion of your readers have their own sites or blogs, a simple strapline such as 'if you like this, we'd love you to create a link to it on your blog or post' will maximize the likelihood of them providing you with a backlink.

Use rich snippets to enhance the appearance of search results

You can use rich snippets to include things like star ratings, reviewer names, prices and so on in search results.

Rich snippets can be used to display star ratings, the number of people reviewing a product or service, pricing information and much else besides. They can help your site stick out in search results.

These can make them more immediately useful to users and more likely to be clicked on – and with clickthrough rate potentially being a ranking signal, their use can improve your search results over time.

You can add rich snippets in two ways – by adding structured markup[40] to the code of your site or using Google's Data Highlighter tool.[41]

Chapter summary

You can ensure that your on-page SEO is robust by following the below steps:

---

40 https://developers.google.com/search/docs/guides/intro-structured-data

41 https://www.google.com/webmasters/tools/data-highlighter

- Use short, search-friendly URLs for your site pages.
- Start your page titles with your keywords.
- Expand your page titles with helpful 'long-tail' keywords.
- Make sure that your H1 tags contains your target keyword.
- Ensure your page titles and H1 tags are unique.
- Write compelling meta-descriptions.
- Include your target keyword in the first paragraph of your page content.
- Include your target keyword in some H2s.
- Include your target keyword a few times in your body copy.
- Make sure your content is fairly long – ideally over 1000 words.
- Increase dwell time by including useful videos, images and infographics on your pages.
- Add some 'LSI keywords' to your pages and posts.

- Ensure you add alt text to your images which contains your target keywords.
- Add links from your pages to relevant, authoritative websites.
- Create relevant internal links on your pages.
- Encourage social sharing of your content.
- Encourage visitors to comment on your posts.
- Add rich snippets to your content to enhance its appearance in search results and improve its clickthrough rate.

6 The technical side of SEO

So far, we've looked fairly exclusively at the content side of SEO: researching what sort of content to produce, creating it and fine-tuning it.

But there's another way that you can improve your position in search results, by making sure that the technical aspects of your website are up to scratch.

By getting the technical setup of your site right, you can make a significant difference to where it appears in search results, and in this chapter, we go through the key tasks you – or more likely the developer working on your website – need to perform.

Use SSL if possible

Secure Sockets Layer – SSL – is a security technology which creates an encrypted link between a web server and a browser. In layman's terms, this means that data sent from your website visitors' browsers (for example, via a form on your site) to your web server is scrambled (encrypted), making it harder for hackers to intercept and make use of this data.[42]

---

[42] It should be noted that SSL is actually something of a 'catch all' term for the protocol involved in making a website secure. Technically speaking a protocol called 'TLS' ('Transport Layer Security') is used nowadays to secure websites, but most people still refer to the technology as SSL.

You can spot a site using SSL fairly easily: the website URL starts with 'https://' rather than 'http://.'

In 2014 Google announced that they wanted to see 'HTTPS everywhere', and that secure HTTPS websites were going to be given preference over non-secure ones in search results.[43]

SSL as a ranking factor was initially described by Google as 'a very lightweight signal', but the indications are that it is becoming more significant (and, SEO considerations aside, the major browsers are now notifying users when a website is not secure in more obvious ways – something that will undermine your users' trust in your site). [44]

So it makes sense, where possible, to ensure your site is secure – this can be done by installing an SSL certificate on your website.[45]

Depending on the platform your site is built on this can be either a straightforward or difficult task – if in doubt about how to enable SSL on your set up, seek professional advice.

---

43 https://webmasters.googleblog.com/2014/08/https-as-ranking-signal.html

44 https://searchengineland.com/google-emails-warnings-webmasters-chrome-will-mark-http-pages-forms-not-secure-280907

45 https://www.verisign.com/en_US/website-presence/website-optimization/ssl-certificates/index.xhtml

If you're building a new website on a brand-new domain, there is no real argument about making it secure from day one. Not only will you be gaining a positive ranking signal, but your users will enjoy a safer browsing experience.

However, if you have an existing website that you want to make secure, **you should tread very carefully**. There are quite a few pitfalls to avoid when making a site secure, and getting the transition from non-secure to secure wrong can considerably damage your site from an SEO point of view.

If you are moving an existing site to SSL, always

- read Google's advice on how to secure your site without damaging your position in search[46]
- involve professionals as and when necessary with the technical work.

I'd also suggest taking a look at Search Engine Land's 'An SEO's guide to securing a website' article, which contains a very useful checklist on all the things you should do to ensure that you don't take a hit in search results.[47]

---

[46] https://support.google.com/webmasters/answer/6073543?hl=en

[47] https://searchengineland.com/http-https-seos-guide-securing-website-246940

Ensure your website is mobile-friendly

In 2016, mobile and tablet internet usage overtook desktop usage for the first time.[48] Google has responded to this growing use of smartphones and tablets by giving websites that are optimized for mobile devices preferential treatment in search results.

Most importantly, this means you need a website that is 'responsive' – i.e., adjusts itself automatically so that it can be navigated and read easily on any device. Google is clear about the fact that having a responsive site is considered a very significant ranking signal by its algorithms.[49]

On top of that, you need to ensure that you follow some other best practices when it comes to optimizing your site for mobile search results:

Don't use Flash

Most phones block Flash and not all search engines index it. Use HTML5 instead if you need to add special effects to your website.

---

48 http://gs.statcounter.com/press/mobile-and-tablet-internet-usage-exceeds-desktop-for-first-time-worldwide

49 https://webmasters.googleblog.com/2016/03/continuing-to-make-web-more-mobile.html

Avoid intrusive 'interstitials' on the mobile version of your site

Popups and interstitials (large banners encouraging people to take particular actions whilst they are browsing your site) are frowned upon by Google, particularly when used on a mobile version of a website.

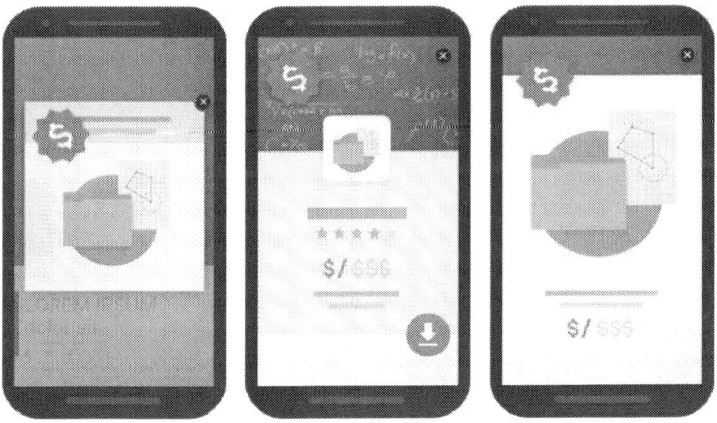

These three images are from Google's guidelines on use of pop-ups and interstitials. The first is an example of an intrusive pop-up; the other two are demonstrations of intrusive interstitials.

Popups relating to legal issues (checking user age, announcing cookie usage etc.) are generally okay, but very intrusive pop-ups encouraging people to buy something or join a mailing list are not.

For a full overview of the SEO implications of interstitials on mobile devices, it's worth taking a look at Google's article on helping users easily access content on mobile devices.[50]

Enable AMP (Accelerated Mobile Pages) where relevant.

AMP is a Google-backed project which aims to speed up the delivery of content on mobile devices through the use of special code known as AMP HTML. [51]

AMP versions of your web pages load extremely quickly on mobile devices. They do this by stripping your content and code down to the bare bones, leaving text, images and video intact but disabling scripts, comments and forms.

Because they load so fast, AMP versions of pages are far more likely to be read and shared by your users, increasing dwell time and the number of backlinks pointing to your content – all good things from an SEO point of view. On top of that, Google sometimes highlights AMP pages in prominent carousels in search results – an important search bump.

Because AMP disables a lot of features and functionality you may

---

[50] https://webmasters.googleblog.com/2016/08/helping-users-easily-access-content-on.html

[51] https://www.ampproject.org/learn/overview/

find that AMP is not right for every page on your site. For news articles and blog posts it generally works superbly, however.

Use Google's tools for assessing how mobile-friendly your site is

You can use Google's Mobile Friendly Test[52] and its Mobile Usability Report[53] to identify any improvements than you need to make to your website to ensure best performance on a mobile device.

Speed your site up

Google really likes websites and pages that load quickly – the company is on record as saying as much.[54]

And site visitors love fast websites too – particularly if they're using mobile devices, where there is an expectation for your content to load very quickly indeed.

If your page loads too slowly, the percentage of people reading, engaging with and sharing your content dips, all of which can have a negative impact on search results (particularly for mobile users).

---

52 https://search.google.com/test/mobile-friendly

53 https://support.google.com/webmasters/answer/6101188?hl=en

54 https://webmasters.googleblog.com/2010/04/using-site-speed-in-web-search-ranking.html

There are several ways you can speed up your site:

Use fast hosting

How fast your site loads depends hugely on the server it's hosted on. Now in some cases – for example if you're using a hosted e-commerce solution like Shopify or Bigcommerce to host your site – you won't have any choice around your hosting provider. But if you are using a self-hosted CMS like WordPress, Drupal or Joomla, then where you host your site is up to you.

If you are going down the self-hosted route, always avoid cheap 'shared hosting' services if possible and use dedicated server hardware and software instead ('managed hosting'). Doing so can boost your site speed significantly and can contribute to a better placement in search results.

Use a fast DNS ('domain name system') provider

You can think of a DNS provider as bit like a phone operator patching through a call. When visitors enter your site's domain name into a browser, your site contacts your DNS provider in order to translate a 'human' web address like www.yoursite.com into an IP address like 123.45.678.9 – this IP address then tells the browser where your site is located.

There is quite some variation amongst DNS providers regarding how long it takes for this process to happen, and although the differences involve only milliseconds, in very competitive niches, a few milliseconds may count for quite a lot in the battle for good search rankings.

The DNSPerf website helps you pick a good provider by showing you how quickly leading DNS companies typically resolve a query.[55]

The above figures from the DNSPerf website highlight the fact that there is quite a large variation (relatively speaking of course!) in the query speed of leading DNS providers.

---

55 http://www.dnsperf.com/

Keep HTTP requests to a minimum

Most of a web page's load time is spent downloading individual components of a page – for example, images, stylesheets and scripts. Every time it loads one of these components, it makes a 'HTTP request' – and you should try to reduce the number of these requests as much as you can.

This means

- only using images and videos on your content that add value to it
- using one CSS file instead of several (we discuss CSS in more depth below)
- reducing the number of scripts in use
- reducing the number of plugins in use.

Be smart with CSS

CSS stands for Cascading Style Sheets – it's code which tells a browser how to display the elements on your web pages. This code is used to control the style of things like text (for example, which typeface should be used), menu bars (what colour and width they should be), images (whether or not there should be a shadow underneath them) ... and so on. You can style any element on your website using CSS.

If implemented correctly, CSS can provide many benefits – the design of every single page on your website can be tweaked by making simple changes to just one file; your site can become more accessible to visually-impaired visitors; and the time it takes to load can be reduced, which can help improve SEO.

CSS can be used either via an external style sheet or inline. An external CSS stylesheet is a standalone file which contains the design instructions for all your web pages (a template, basically). This is then loaded by your web pages to apply the design. Using CSS inline, by contrast, involves the addition of CSS code directly to each web page.

To ensure that your site loads quickly, and thus gets the SEO juice associated with good site speed, *always* use an external stylesheet and avoid inline CSS. Inline CSS makes the code on your web pages significantly 'heavier' and slower to load.

Additionally, it's important to try to only use *one* CSS style sheet. Some designers like working with multiple CSS files but it is better from an SEO point of view to combine them into one. This minimizes the number of HTTP requests being made (see above) and makes your site load more quickly.

Finally, it's a good idea to use CSS instead of images where possible.[56] This is because every image you add to a web page creates a HTTP request (which as discussed above, we want to keep to a minimum). There are quite a few contexts where instead of using an actual image on a web page, you can program it into the CSS – things like buttons, gradients, drop shadows and even logos can be created using CSS.[57]

Enable compression on your website

Earlier we discussed the importance of 'long-form content' in SEO – but this can make the file sizes of your pages quite large. Using compression on your site can reduce the bandwidth used by your pages, meaning that they load quicker. You can compress pages with a tool called Gzip.[58]

Minify your site's code

Every unnecessary piece of code increases the size of your web pages – so it makes sense to streamline it as much as possible.

This means getting rid of any unnecessary spaces, line breaks or indentation in your HTML, CSS and Javascript. There are many

---

[56] https://robertnyman.com/2010/04/21/using-css-instead-of-images-when-coding-your-web-design/

[57] https://css-tricks.com/create-your-logo-with-pure-css/

[58] http://www.gnu.org/software/gzip/

tools available to help you do this – I'd suggest you check out Google's 'Minify Resources' guide for details.[59]

Optimize your images

The smaller your image files are, the faster your pages will load. Here are some key ways you can reduce image size:

- **Crop your images** to suit the width of your page (i.e., if your page is 1000px wide, use a 1000px wide image rather than uploading an image that is 2000px wide and rescaling it using the 'width' parameter).

- **Use JPGs** as your file type wherever possible. (Always avoid uploading BMPs and TIFFs).

- **Compress your images** as much as you can – obviously you need to be careful here, because you don't want to use images which are so compressed and pixelated that they make your content look amateurish. Tools like Tinypng can help in this regard.[60]

---

59 https://developers.google.com/speed/docs/insights/MinifyResources

60 https://tinypng.com/

Fix duplicate content issues

It's important to avoid publishing duplicate content on your site – or, where this is not possible, telling Google which one to prioritize.

Why duplicate content causes problems

A key reason why you need to avoid publishing duplicate content is to do with backlinks. Remember that at the simplest level, a backlink counts as a vote for a piece of content. If you have a great piece of content, but two versions of it on your site, you may end up getting some external links to one version, some to the other. This effectively 'splits your vote' and dilutes the value of these backlinks.

To illustrate this, say you and your competitor are both writing an article about the health benefits of baked beans. He gets 10 backlinks to his piece. You get 6 backlinks to version A of yours, and 6 to your version B. Despite you getting more backlinks in total to your content than your competitor did to his, in this situation your competitor would quite possibly outrank you in search results, simply because his piece of content has more votes for it than either of yours. (Obviously, other factors – such as the quality of the backlinks in question, the anchor text used etc. – would come into play, but you get the idea).

A lot of the time, duplicate content is not created on purpose – your content management system (CMS) or developer, rather than you personally, is often the culprit. Depending on the system you're using to publish content, you may find that in certain contexts it creates multiple versions of URLs which involve additional parameters and 'session IDs'.

A classic example of this is the printer-friendly version of a piece of content – you might publish an article on your site only to see two versions of it appear:

www.mysite.com/baked-beans
www.mysite.com/baked-beans?format=print

The first version might be the 'heavy' one – containing images, banner ads, comments, sharing icons etc...and the second version might be a lighter version, with all the 'fluff' stripped away for printing / paper-saving purposes.

Google then has to make a choice between which of these two versions to index – and given what we've discussed above, it might well prioritize the cleaner, printer-friendly version (which might be not be at all ideal from your perspective).

Preventing duplicate content from appearing

To avoid ending up with multiple versions of the same page or post, the first thing you need to do is switch off any options in your CMS that generate duplicate content – this usually means disabling Session IDs where they are not vital to the functionality of your website and getting rid of printer-friendly pages.

Where your CMS is *not* the culprit, the problem can usually be traced back to you or your developer.

For example, you might be publishing duplicate or extremely similar versions of an article on purpose (in which case, stop it!) or creating multiple URLs to serve as tracking links for different marketing channels – i.e.,

www.mysite.com/article?source=facebook
www.mysite.com/article?source=radio
www.mysite.com/article?source=tv

etc.

This in effect creates multiple versions of the same content – all of which get crawled by Google (which in turn has to choose which one is the authoritative one, and sometimes in a way which might not be beneficial to your business). A way around this is to use hash marks (#) instead - i.e., www.mysite.com/article#radio.

(You can find a useful overview of how to go about working with SEO-friendly tracking links on the SEO Adjust website.)[61]

---

[61] http://www.seoadjust.com/web-analytics/seo-friendly-google-analytics-campaign-tracking-with-hash-marks/

If you find that your website is producing multiple URLs for the same page or post, and you can't find a setting to disable this, your developer may have hard coded something into your site's setup – in which case, have a chat with him/her to see what can be done to rectify this.

Important note: if your site has been creating multiple URLs of the same page or post for a while, some of these may have links from other sites pointing to them. Accordingly, these URLs, despite generating duplicate content, may have an SEO value – and remember: every (quality) backlink is a vote for your content and boosts its position in search.

It's therefore highly important that you never remove an existing URL without creating a '301 redirect' to the preferred version of the page. A 301 redirect – also known as a 'permanent redirect' tells Google where the deleted content has moved to.[62]

The process involved with creating 301 redirects varies by CMS and site setup, so I can't give specific instructions here – if in doubt about how to create these redirects, speak to your developer.

---

62 https://moz.com/learn/seo/redirection

Telling Google which version of a page to prioritize

There are instances where you simply can't get rid of a duplicate version of a page (or there is a valid business reason for keeping it in existence).

In these cases, it's advisable to use the 'canonical link element' to let search engines know where the preferred version of your content resides.[63]

This usually involves adding a line of HTML <head> section of your website, detailing the main version of your page or post.

```
<head>
  <link rel="canonical" href="http://example.com/preferred-content" />
</head>
```

Create an XML sitemap

An XML sitemap is a file that helps Google to understand your website whilst crawling it – you can think of it as being like a roadmap for search engines.

---

63 https://en.wikipedia.org/wiki/Canonical_link_element

Above all else, a sitemap lets Google know the location of each page on your site; this is particularly important for new sites (which won't have any external links pointing Google to your content).

It also contains useful information about each page on your site, including

- when it was last modified;
- what priority it has on your site;
- how frequently it is updated.

There are several tools available which you can use to create a sitemap for your site – a list of suggestions is available from Google on their Google Code project.[64]

Once you've created your sitemap, you need to submit it to Google via its Search Console tool, which we discuss below.

Register your site with Google Search Console

Google Search Console is a free tool from Google that allows you to submit your website to Google for indexing.[65] To register your site

---

64 https://code.google.com/archive/p/sitemap-generators/wikis/SitemapGenerators.wiki

65 https://www.google.com/webmasters/tools/home?hl=en

properly with Search Console, there are three main steps you need to take.

1. Add each version of your website

First you need to add each variation of your 'root URL' to Search Console.[66] This means creating a 'property' in Search Console for both the www and non-www version of your site, as well as the secure and non-secure versions. Typically this means you end up registering four URLs in Search console, i.e.,

http://www.yourdomain.com
http://yourdomain.com
https://www.yourdomain.com
https://yourdomain.com

2. Verify your site

As part of the process of adding each variant, you will need to verify ownership of each of them.[67]

There are a quite a few different ways to do this – these include uploading a file to your site; adding some HTML to the <head> section of your home page; using Google Analytics; or adding a text record to your DNS settings. These choices are highlighted – and

[66] https://support.google.com/webmasters/answer/34592
[67] https://support.google.com/webmasters/answer/9008080

relevant instructions provided – as you go through the process of adding each property.

3. Submit your sitemap

Once you've added all your properties to Search Console, you need to submit your XML sitemap for all of them.[68] This is very easy to do – you just go to each property, and then click on the Sitemaps section in the dashboard.

Use Search Console to improve site performance

Although Search Console provides a great way to notify Google of your site's existence, it does far more than that and is vital to the long-term success of an SEO project.

Using Search Console you can also:

- check how many backlinks to your site there are, and where they originate from
- ensure that Google is not experiencing any crawl errors with your site
- let Google know if different versions of your websites exist for different countries
- check that your site is fully usable on a mobile device

---

[68] https://support.google.com/webmasters/answer/183668?hl=en

- view the kinds of search queries that are driving traffic to your site
- 'disavow' spammy backlinks which may be damaging your site's performance in search results
- add rich snippets and rich cards – containing star ratings, author information, prices, images – to your search results (the presence of this additional information often leads to a higher clickthrough rate to your content).

As such, you can use Search Console *regularly* to ensure that your site is performing as it should and to access important data which can inform your SEO strategy.

For an in-depth overview of how to use Google Search Console to maximum effect, I'd suggest reading Google's own guide to using Google Search Console as a powerful SEO tool – it goes through each of the Search Console features in considerable depth and shows you how to completely integrate Search Console into your SEO work.[69]

I also discuss the features of Search Console in more depth later in this book – in Chapter 11, 'Maintaining your site's performance in search results.'

---

69 https://support.google.com/webmasters/?hl=en#topic=9128571

Add Google Analytics to your site

Another key Google service you need to create an account for – and add to your site – is Google Analytics.

Google Analytics provides you with in-depth statistics on traffic to your website. Some key metrics include:

1. How many people are accessing each piece of content on your site
2. How your visitors discovered your content (i.e., via searching, a social media link, a paid advert etc.)
3. What search queries led to visits to particular pages
4. How long it takes a particular piece of content to load
5. How long they stayed on a particular page.

All of the above pieces of information help you tweak your site so that it performs well in search.

The first two metrics allows you identify the pages that are performing well in organic search, and which need attention.

The third metric allows you to get valuable data on the keywords which are driving traffic successfully – or identify keywords that should be performing better.

The fourth metric allows you to spot pages that are loading more slowly than they should and make technical or content changes to speed them up accordingly (remember: Google hates slow-loading pages).

The fifth metric allows you to evaluate the quality of content on individual pages. If your users are leaving a particular page quickly, that's a sign that it's not answering their query – or solving their problem – adequately, and as such needs improvement. This is because, as discussed earlier, Google likes to see a long 'dwell time' on your site's pages: the longer, the better from an SEO point of view.

Chapter summary

To ensure that your site performs as well as possible in search results, you need to set it up correctly from a technical point of view. This means following the below steps:

- Use SSL on your site if possible.
- Ensure you use a responsive website which performs well on mobile devices.
- Use the fastest hosting provider you can.
- Use the fastest DNS provider you can.

- Avoid use of pop ups and interstitials, particularly on mobile devices.

- Don't use Flash.

- Enable AMP (accelerated mobile pages).

- Keep HTTPs requests to a minimum by removing non-essential scripts and content from your site's pages.

- Be smart with CSS - use one CSS stylesheet to cater for your website's design and avoid use of inline CSS.

- Enable compression on your website.

- Minify your site's code.

- Optimize all your images via cropping and compression.

- Fix any duplicate content issues.

- Create an XML sitemap.

- Register your site with Google Search Console, and use it regularly to analyse your site's performance in search results.

- Add Google Analytics to your site and check key metrics regularly to identify improvements you can make to improve your site's search ranking.

7 Creating backlinks to your site

At this point in proceedings you've ticked some very important SEO boxes: you've put some great content based on solid keyword research together and taken key steps on the technical side to ensure that it's presented as well as it possibly can be to search engines.

However, it's unlikely that you've got much in the way of organic search traffic yet, because you're still missing a crucial ingredient: **backlinks**.

What are backlinks, and why do they matter?

Backlinks are simply links from other people's sites to yours; and they matter because Google treats them as votes for your content.[70] The more links you get for a particular page, the greater your chance of it being 'elected' – i.e., becoming visible in search results.

An important thing to remember however is that some backlinks are 'worth' considerably more than others. A backlink from *The New York Times* website to yours, for example, is treated *very* differently by Google to a backlink you might have received from a not-very-well-known blogger.

[70] https://en.wikipedia.org/wiki/Backlink

This is because *The New York Times* has millions of links pointing to it – making it a very authoritative website – and your blogger friend's site doesn't.

As you might therefore expect, that link from *The New York Times* to your site gives your content a much greater boost in search results than the one from the small-time blogger.

Some backlinks can, in fact, *hurt* your site's chances of performing well in search results.

If you use a spammy approach to link building – for example by posting links on a bunch of gambling forums to a site which has absolutely nothing to do with gambling, Google is likely to interpret this as a scattergun, spammy approach to backlink building – and demote you in search results as a result.

All this means that you don't just need to build backlinks for your site, but build 'good backlinks.'

What makes a 'good' backlink'?

As I've indicated above, not all backlinks are created equal – some are considerably more useful than others, and it's important to understand the difference between 'good' and 'bad' backlinks.

Typically, a good backlink will display the following characteristics:

1. It's on a high-quality website

You should always aim to avoid getting backlinks on low-authority websites. If lots of sites with bad reputations are linking to yours, this can damage your position in search results (this is why you should always avoid 'paid link' services).

Conversely, if you can get backlinks from high-quality websites, this can turbo-charge your site's performance in search results. Examples of websites that can provide a lot of 'link juice' (ranking power) if they contain a backlink to your website include:

- websites run by educational institutions (.edu, .ac.uk)
- government websites (.gov., .gov.uk)
- influential blogs
- newspaper websites

To find out how authoritative – or high quality - a website is, you can turn to your keyword research tool.

This will give you a quality-indicating 'domain score' for any URL you enter into it, along with a list of the backlinks pointing to that domain (and their domain scores).

2. It make sense in context

When evaluating backlinks, Google's algorithms pay particular attention to context. If a backlink to your article about self-driving cars features in an article about baked beans, then Google will not take it particularly seriously – and may even view it as spam (and penalize your site accordingly).

Ideally, if you're on a quest for backlinks, you should target websites featuring content topics that are similar or related to yours.

3. It contains informative anchor text

It's generally helpful if your backlinks contain some information about the content they are linking to. This can be achieved through the inclusion of keywords in anchor text (the clickable text in a hyperlink).

So, for example, if an influential blogger agrees to place a link to your article about self-driving cars in one of his/her posts, it's much more valuable if you can persuade him/her to use the phrase 'self-driving cars' in the anchor text instead of something like 'read more here.'

Like much else in SEO however, it's possible to overdo anchor text optimization to the point where Google's algorithms start considering your manipulation of anchor text as a spammy – so it's advisable, where you have a say in such matters, to avoid suggesting the *exact* same anchor text repeatedly to any webmasters giving you an anchor text.

Mix it up a little – in the example above, you could occasionally suggest 'self-driving vehicles', 'autonomous cars', 'driverless cars' as anchor text too.

4. It is a 'dofollow' link

When creating a link to a URL, webmasters can specify that search engines follow (and index) that link or not, by using 'dofollow' or 'nofollow' attributes in the link's HTML code.

If 'dofollow' is used, the backlink (as the name suggests) is followed, and it counts as a vote of confidence for the URL in question – 'nofollow' by contrast stops this from happening.

So, when you are reaching out to webmasters for link-building purposes, always try to get 'dofollow' links wherever possible.

What makes a 'bad' backlink?

Just as a high-quality backlink can improve your position in search, a 'bad' one can hurt your SEO efforts. Google's algorithm prioritizes 'natural' links (generated by real people) over links which are created using underhand or automated methods.

To ensure that you don't generate any low-quality backlinks, always avoid what Google refer to as 'link schemes', which the company describes as:

- Buying or selling links that pass PageRank.[71] This includes exchanging money for links, or posts that contain links; exchanging goods or services for links; or sending someone a "free" product in exchange for them writing about it and including a link

- Excessive link exchanges ("Link to me and I'll link to you") or partner pages exclusively for the sake of cross-linking

- Large-scale article marketing or guest posting campaigns with keyword-rich anchor text links

- Using automated programs or services to create links to your site

The above information is from Google's dedicated Search Console resource on the topic (where you can read more about link schemes).[72]

Link building tactics

It's one thing having an understanding of what a 'good' backlink constitutes; quite another to actually get your hands on one! Let's

[71] https://en.wikipedia.org/wiki/PageRank

[72] https://support.google.com/webmasters/answer/66356?hl=en

take a look at some of the key link-building tactics that you can employ to generate links.

Create quality content

As discussed in Chapter 4, Google loves quality content – its increasingly sophisticated algorithms are more and more adept at understanding language and spotting articles that genuinely solve users' problems.

That's why – irrespective of the number of links to them – great posts can sometimes receive preferential treatment in Google search results.

It's not just Google that rewards quality content however – readers do too, and the way they do so is by creating a backlink to it on another website – and well, bingo.

Either they do this by adding a link from their website to yours, or, more commonly, by sharing your content on social networks (believe it or not, not everybody has a website!).

The first method of backlink creation – where somebody links to your site from theirs – is, from an SEO point of view, technically more important to you. This is because backlinks from conventional sites to each other tend are more likely to be 'dofollow' than the links created by social shares.

However, social shares do have an indirect SEO value, because they result in more people eyeballing your content (and potentially more backlink creation and social shares happening – a nice little virtuous circle can kick in).

So, in a nutshell, a great piece of content can do an awful lot of the heavy lifting for you. Once it starts to get some traffic, it can (to a degree) automatically generate lots of the 'natural links' that Google loves, simply as a result of its inherently viral nature.

The trick is, of course, getting it that traffic in the first place, and that's where you've got to start looking beyond your own website and actively trying to secure links to your content on other people's.

Perform email outreach

Email outreach, as the name suggests, means getting in touch with other site owners, asking them to put a link to your content in theirs. In my experience it works best when you include both personal contacts and people you don't know in the process.

Personal contacts

The first group of site owners I'd suggest you contact is people you know – it's likely that you have some contacts who run websites, and they might be able to feature a link to your site somewhere on theirs.

For example, if you're a web designer, you may find that your clients are happy to include a 'built by *YourCompany*' link somewhere on their site. This can have some value, particularly if you have built websites that have a lot of external links pointing to them.

It's better however if the link makes sense in context – i.e., perhaps sympathetic contacts might be encouraged to post news of your site going live in a blog post, along with a description of what your business does and reasons why their audience might visit it.

The ideal scenario is when your contacts have written blog posts about the specific business area you work in (or the kind of thing you're writing about on your blog) and they can be convinced to include a link to your content in those posts.

You may find that by working your personal contacts, you can build up quite a few useful backlinks with fairly minimal effort – and you'd be surprised at the effect that this can have on your search results, particularly if you have some clients or contacts with authoritative websites.

But in order to *really* scale things up, you're going to have to get in touch with some people you don't know.

Unsolicited contacts

In order to get a large number of sites linking to your site, you are usually going to have to do some 'cold' email outreach and ask people that you have no relationship at all with for a backlink.

This is a time-consuming (and if we're honest, not terribly enjoyable) process, so it's important to find the right people to pester.

The simplest way to go about finding the right site owners to approach is as follows:

1. Find out what the number one result is for your focus keyword.
2. Get a list of the sites linking to that top result.
3. Contact the owners of those sites, asking for a link in a relevant part of their site.

To find out the number one result for your focus keyword, you just need to search for it in Google.

To get a list of the sites linking to that top result, you need to use a keyword research tool – this is usually a case of pasting the URL of the top-ranking result into the backlinks analysis section of your chosen tool (Ahrefs, Moz, Serpstat etc.) and getting a list of the sites linking to your competitor's content.

To contact all the site owners, you'll need their contact details. If they are not immediately available from their website, you can – as SEO expert Brian Dean suggests[73] – use tools such as Hunter.io[74] and Voila Nobert[75] to find the relevant details quickly.

Dean also suggests using personalized 'scripts' to speed up the process of email outreach – where you use the same text each time.

This apparently is his best performing script:

> Hi [First Name],
>
> I was looking for content on [Topic] today, when I stumbled on your article: [Article Title].
>
> Good stuff! I especially enjoyed [Something specific from their article].
>
> Also, I just published a new guide on [Your Topic]: [URL].

---

73 https://backlinko.com/link-building#chapter4

74 https://hunter.io/

75 https://www.voilanorbert.com/

As someone that writes about [Topic], I thought you'd enjoy it.

My guide may also make a nice addition to your page. Either way, keep up the awesome work with [Website]!

Talk Soon,
[Your Name]

Theoretically, you could further speed all this up by using email marketing tools (Getresponse,[76] Aweber,[77] Mailchimp etc.[78]) to send mass mailouts – but doing so may be in breach of data protection laws in your territory, so tread carefully here.

Of course, if this type of outreach seems like too much work, and you have a suitable budget, you could always pay somebody to take care of it for you. You have to be very careful about who you commission though, because the internet is full of SEO 'experts' who use very dubious tactics to build backlinks — tactics that can actively hurt your website's position in search results.

---

[76] https://www.stylefactoryproductions.com/blog/getresponse-review

[77] https://www.stylefactoryproductions.com/blog/aweber-review

[78] https://mailchimp.com/

If you end up paying for link-building services, only use a reputable SEO company or consultant — otherwise you may end up being penalized by Google for having a lot of low-quality, spammy links pointing to your website. (We discuss penalties and how to recover from them in more depth in Chapter 11).

Guest post

Guest posting – writing articles on other people's blogs – is a bit of a funny one.

It can definitely be used as a way to improve your position in search, but you have to be careful about how you go about it.

This is chiefly because Google is on record as saying it doesn't like guest blogging as a way of acquiring links – in an article on the topic, Matt Cutts, former head of Google's Webspam team, had this to say about it:

> Stick a fork in it: guest blogging is done; it's just gotten too spammy. In general I wouldn't recommend accepting a guest blog post unless you are willing to vouch for someone personally or know them well. Likewise, I wouldn't recommend relying on guest posting, guest

> blogging sites, or guest blogging SEO as a link building strategy.[79]

In the same article, however, he rows back a bit on this:

> There are still many good reasons to do some guest blogging (exposure, branding, increased reach, community, etc.). Those reasons existed way before Google and they'll continue into the future. And there are absolutely some fantastic, high-quality guest bloggers out there.

The takeaways from this is, in my view, are as follows:

- Don't overdo guest blog posts.
- Only contribute guest blog posts to genuinely authoritative sites.
- When you contribute a blog post, make sure it contains in-depth, genuinely useful content – the sort that you'd be happy to publish on your own site.
- Don't stuff your guest posts full of links containing over-optimized anchor text.

In other words: if somebody offers you a chance to contribute to *The New York Times*, go for it.

---

[79] https://www.mattcutts.com/blog/guest-blogging/

If somebody asks you to write for a saucy blog that has no domain authority and nothing to do with your business area, then forget about it.

Issue a press release

If you are launching a new product or service, you may be able to build up some backlinks on relevant sites quickly by distributing a press release to journalists and bloggers who cover the industry you work in.

If they like the sound of your product, they might be inclined to cover it on the sites they write for (and crucially, provide a link back to your site on their article).

There are a couple of ways to go about this: first, you can hire a PR agency to both craft and distribute your press release. If you're doing this, make sure the company you use definitely has the right contacts for your field.

The second way is to distribute press releases is do it yourself. This basically means distributing a press release via syndication sites such as iReach[80] and Businesswire;[81] you'll need to do some research however, to find out what sites are the best ones to use for your niche.

---

80 https://ireach.prnewswire.com/Home.aspx

81 https://www.businesswire.com/portal/site/home/

Whichever path you take, you should ensure that your press release

- is extremely-well written;
- is distributed to relevant sites;
- contains a link to a page containing information about the product.

Engage in broken link building

Broken link building involves getting webmasters on sites containing broken links (URLs that can't resolve or return a 404 error) to replace them with a backlink to your content.

There are generally three steps involved in this:

- Finding a broken link on a website;
- Recreating that 'broken content' (or identifying a piece of existing content on your site that would make a good replacement destination for the broken link);
- Asking webmasters to replace the broken link on their site with a link to your content.

This is a very effective method of generating new and valuable backlinks to your site – particularly if you can find a page which is no longer accessible but has a lot of links pointing to it.

Each stage of broken link building can be an arduous, time consuming task. Fortunately, however, there are tools available to help you automate the process.

For example, you can enter a competitor's website into Ahrefs and see a list of broken links to it.[82] Then, you can reach out to the owners of the sites with the broken links, suggesting your content instead.

Broken Link Builder is another tool that can really speed up the process – particularly where identifying contact details for the owners of sites containing broken links is concerned.[83]

For a detailed overview of how to carry out broken link building, I'd suggest taking a look at Moz's two detailed articles on the subject:

- The Broken Link Building Bible[84]
- Broken Link Building Bible: The New Testament[85]

Submit your site to directories

Submitting your site to online directories can be a way of generating backlinks and gaining an SEO benefit – but only if you

---

[82] https://ahrefs.com/dashboard/metrics

[83] http://brokenlinkbuilding.com/

[84] https://moz.com/blog/the-broken-link-building-bible

[85] https://moz.com/blog/broken-link-building-bible-new-testament

choose the right ones. If you submit your site to a low-quality, spammy directory, you can do more harm than good to it.

The key things to remember when submitting a site to a directory are:

- Only submit to high quality directories which have an editorial team.
- Focus only on directories which list sites in your niche.
- Never use automated directory submission services.

Search Engine Journal provides some useful pointers on directory submissions, along with a list of some high-quality directories.[86]

Make a useful web tool

If you can create something that performs a task and saves people time (and make a little bit of noise about it), you can end up with a lot of backlinks.

Examples include:

- free privacy policies
- tax calculators

---

86 https://www.searchenginejournal.com/directory-submission-sites-google-likes-162689-2/162689/

- URL shorteners
- WordPress plugins
- SEO tools.

Good examples of the above can generate links in a similar way to high quality content; the inherently 'viral' nature of the functionality encourages people to create links to them.

Run a survey – and publish the results

Running a survey can help you generate backlinks – in two ways.

First, it gives you an excuse to reach out to your contacts and ask them to create a link to the page on your site where the survey is hosted.

Second, you can use the data gleaned from the survey to create a high-quality piece of content that you can place on your site (and ask your contacts to link to).

They key thing here is quality: you need to make sure that the survey itself is capturing valuable data, and the way you present the results is extremely interesting.

Use alerts to find new content related to your business area

You can find sites where you might be able to secure a backlink through the use of alerts. Google Alerts is a good starting point for this – you can enter your focus keywords into it and every time it locates an article containing your chosen phrase, it will send you an email with the URL.[87]

You can then follow up with the webmasters of the sites Google has notified you about with a view to getting a backlink placed on them.

Several of the leading keyword research tools offer alert functionality too.

Advertise your content online

The idea of online advertising as a way of boosting the number of links to your site might initially sound rather strange.

However, there are a few ways in which it may help you – albeit in a roundabout way – get some backlinks.

Because of the big brother nature of online advertising – where you can show ads to very precise groups of people, you can put your

---

[87] https://www.google.co.uk/alerts

high-quality content directly in front of the people who are most likely to read it (and by extension, create backlinks to it).

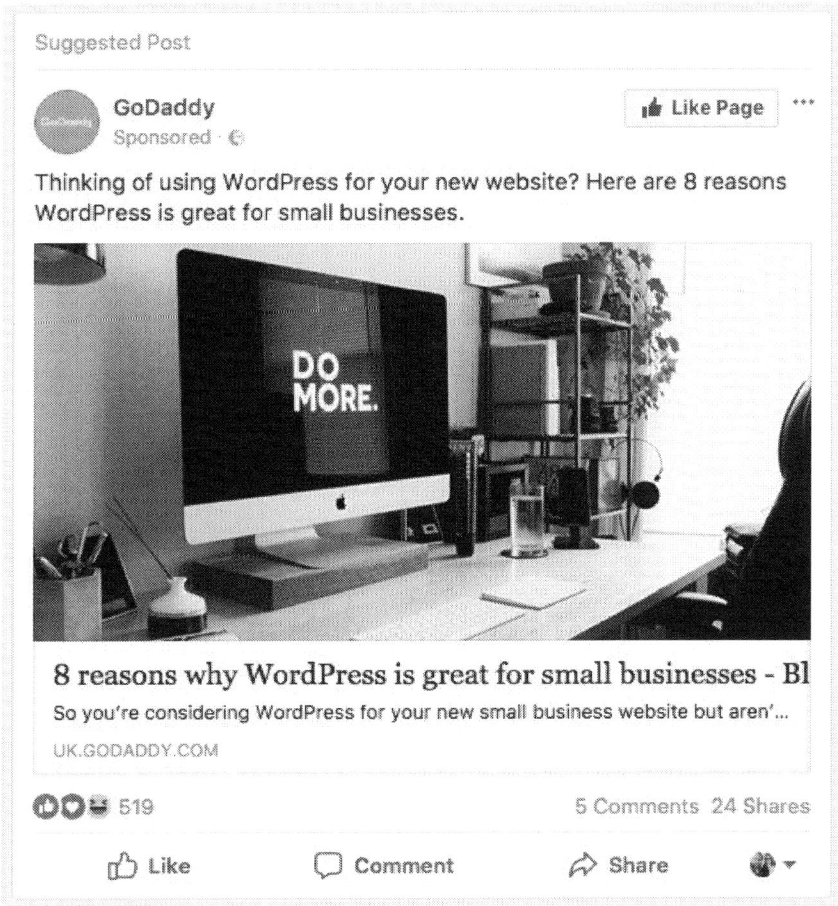

In this Facebook ad, Godaddy is not promoting a service but a blog post.

For example, you could use Facebook advertising to show a 'how to blog' guide to entrepreneurs, or a 'how to promote your band' guide to musicians.

The point is that you can use online advertising to make your content more generally visible to very relevant niche audiences. If you have the budget for it, then it's worth experimenting with online adverts as a way of giving your content 'legs'.

Actively encourage your readers to create backlinks

Depending on the niche you work in, you may find yourself in a position where many of your site visitors run websites themselves.

Many of these will be happy to add a link from their site to yours – particularly if your content is very useful to them. But they might need a little nudge – that's why I suggest ending every post with an encouragement to your readers to create a backlink to your content on their site or blog.

I'd also suggest that you include this call to action in any e-newsletters that you send promoting your latest posts.

Chapter summary

Backlinks

- Backlinks are links from other sites to yours; they a very important ranking signal.

- The more backlinks you have to your site – generally speaking – the better it will perform in search results.

- Some backlinks are more influential in helping your site rank than others – a link from an authoritative site such as *The New York Times* (which has millions of backlinks pointing to it) will boost your site in search results much more than a link from a little-known blog.

- 'Good backlinks' have 4 main characteristics: they are on authoritative websites; they feature on pages which cover the same topic as the page or post being linked to; they contain anchor text containing keywords you'd like to rank for; and they are 'dofollow' links.

- If you want to avoid being penalized by Google in search results, you should always avoid using paid links or link schemes. These are 'bad' backlinks which can damage your position in search results.

Link building tactics

In order to increase the number of backlinks to your site, it is necessary to employ link-building tactics. Some of my key suggestions for doing so are as follows:

- Create quality content – long-form content that is so good that people will *want* to create backlinks to it.

- Perform email outreach – ask both personal contacts and site owners that you don't know to create backlinks to your content.

- Guest post – but carefully. Post only on quality sites, don't over-optimize the anchor text for the links back to your site, and limit the number of backlinks you include in your posts.

- When you launch a new product or service, use a PR agency or press release distribution service to get it featured on sites that are relevant to your industry.

- Use broken link building – find links to content that don't work anymore and try to get the site owners to replace these with links to *your* content.

- Provide free but valuable web tools on your site; if these perform useful tasks, site owners will happily link to pages where they can be downloaded.

- Use web alerts (using tools such as Google Alerts or Ahrefs) to find sites publishing content related to your business area and ask the owners of these for a backlink.

- Run surveys and publish the results – this gives you an opportunity to ask webmasters to feature a link to both the survey and the results on their sites.

- Consider using online advertising to boost the visibility of your content and gain more backlinks to it.

- Issue a clear call to action on your blog posts (and any promotional material about them) to encourage readers to create a backlink to it.

Further reading on backlink creation

Although the above suggestions on how to create backlinks cover the key tactics you should employ, there is a myriad of ways to go about this. Therefore, I would suggest that you dive deeper into this area of SEO by reading some of the articles below:

Moz's guide to link building[88]
Point Blank SEO's exhaustive list of link building tactics[89]
Ahref's 'noob friendly' guide to link building[90]

---

88 https://moz.com/beginners-guide-to-link-building/tactics
89 http://pointblankseo.com/link-building-strategies
90 https://ahrefs.com/blog/link-building/

8 Local SEO – a quick win?

Let's say you run a bike shop.

Now, there are loads of bike shops out there, and typing this phrase into Google will provide a plethora of results.

Amongst these results you'll typically find large chains occupying the top spots – in the UK, where I'm based, stores like Evans, Halfords and Rutland Cycling (all household-name bike retailers) occupy positions in the top 5 search results for this phrase.

Despite this, my local independent bike shop outranks them all and is the first result I see when I search for a bike shop.

Why? Because Google pays huge attention to the geographical location of the searcher, and my local bike shop was smart enough to recognize this and take some simple steps to ensure maximum visibility in the part of London that I live in.

If your business is even more 'niched', the results of local SEO can be even more significant.

As an example of this, one of my SEO clients recently set up a particular type of PR firm in London. As you might expect, this is a niche service, and there are nowhere near as many PR firms in London as there are bike shops. But nonetheless, when I came to do the work on her site, I found some very well-established competitors already occupying the number one spot in Google for searches for her type of business.

Within a few days she outranked them all for any search made for her type of business by users located *anywhere* in London – i.e., not just in the suburb where her office was located.

Again, local SEO was the reason why. Her competitors had not paid sufficient attention to the power of local SEO, and they lost out as a result.

So, what do you need to do to make a site rank highly in local search results?

Register your business with Google My Business

Creating a Google My Business profile takes five minutes, and is one of the easiest things you can do to ensure visibility in search results.[91]

When you set up your profile, you supply your business address to Google. Google then sends a card to your business address containing a PIN which you use to verify the address.

---

[91] https://www.google.co.uk/intl/en/business/

Once that's done, within a couple of days you should see your business included on the map that Google displays when users in your area enter a search for your type of service.

Depending on how many other similar businesses in your area have registered with Google My Business, you may even find yourself occupying the top spot.

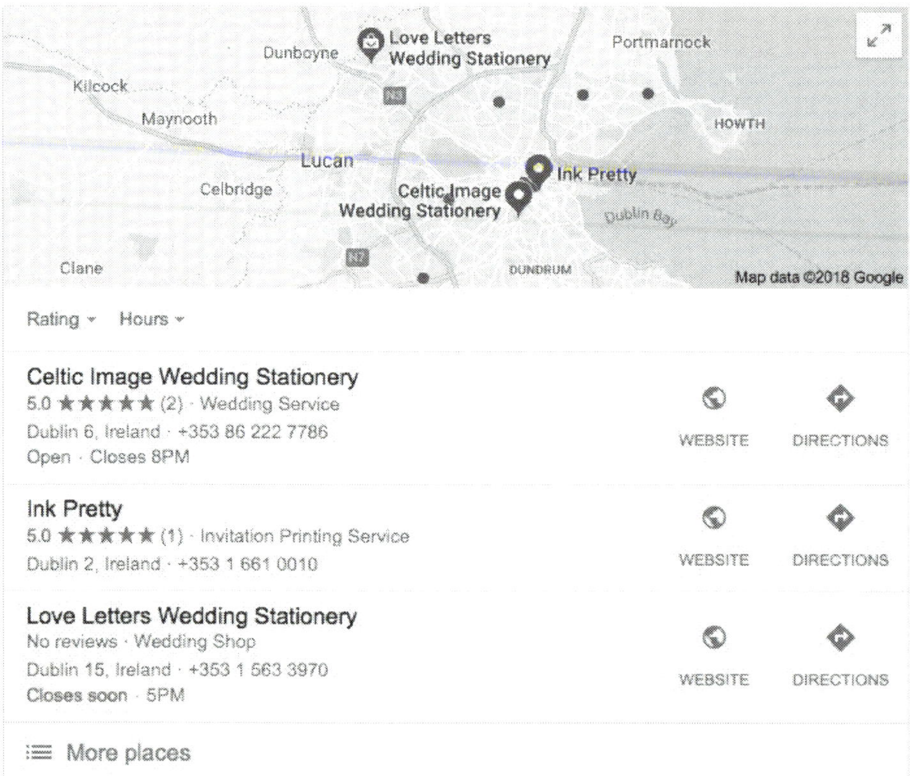

The Google My Business map results are usually placed above regular text-based search results, meaning that if you register your geographical location with Google My Business, you could leapfrog your competitors in the rankings.

If you run a business which has offices in several locations, you should register those in Google My Business too (if you have several locations, you can bulk upload them).[92]

Ensure your location is referenced in key parts of your site

You should make sure that your home page and any other page containing information about your product and service reference your location in four key places:

- its title
- headings and body copy
- its meta description.
- the footer.

Additionally, I'd suggest adding the location in the URL where relevant. For example, if you ran a chain of curry houses, with locations in three parts of London, I'd suggest using three separate URLs, for example:

www.mycurryhouse.co.uk/walthamstow-curry
www.mycurryhouse.co.uk/brixton-curry
www.mycurryhouse.co.uk/hampstead-curry

---

[92] https://support.google.com/business/answer/3217744?hl=en-GB

You'll notice that I put the word 'curry' in there too – this is in case somebody ends up using the whole link as anchor text. As we saw earlier, URLs with keywords in them can help Google categorize your page accurately when your URL is used verbatim by somebody creating a link to your site.

In essence, I would follow all the on-page SEO advice I provided in Chapter 5, but remembering to use your location as part of your focus keyword where applicable.

One thing to bear in mind with this however, is that you might need to think about how wide to cast the net when referencing your location.

For some businesses, perhaps those offering goods and services in a very specific area, it will make sense to take a 'hyper-local' approach – to use the town or suburb they are based in as a focus keyword.

For others, where there is perhaps less competition for the services they provide, or a desire to sell to customers in a wider geographical area, it will make sense to reference the name of a county or state in key parts of their site.

Submit your site to local directories

Submitting your sites to quality local directories can significantly boost your position in search.

First, Google indexes the directory entries – and if the directory is reputable, it may return your directory entry as part of the top 5 results. This means that even if you are struggling to get a high ranking for your site, you may still get visibility for your business in search results.

Second, you may get a backlink out of it, which can enhance general performance in search results.

Third, you will make your business more visible to anyone using those directories.

Seek out online reviews (particularly Google ones)

Google has this to say about reviews on Google My Business:

High-quality, positive reviews from your customers will improve your business's visibility and increase the likelihood that a potential customer will visit your location.[93]

---

93 https://support.google.com/business/answer/7091

In my view, this is a big hint that Google may treat Google My Business reviews as a ranking signal. So, it's important to encourage any customers who are happy with your product or service to leave a review.

You can use Google Place IDs to give your satisfied customers a direct link to a page where they can leave a review – Google provides some useful information on how to do this on their Google My Business Help site.[94]

Not only could these reviews give you a positive ranking signal, but the little stars beside your business name which appear after a customer writes a review will also help your business stick out from the crowd on Google's map results.

Use Schema's geographic markup

You can add Schema's geographic markup to the code of your site which helps search engines better identify your location.

Typically, this involves adding some code like the below to your website:

```
<div itemscope
itemtype="http://schema.org/Attorney">
<span itemprop="name">ABC Attorneys</span>
```

---

94 https://support.google.com/business/answer/7035772

```
<div itemprop="address" itemscope
itemtype="http://schema.org/PostalAddress">
<span itemprop="streetAddress">123 Main
Street</span>
<span itemprop="addressLocality">Malibu</span>,
<span itemprop="addressRegion">CA</span>
<span itemprop="postalCode">90263</span>
</div>
Phone: <span itemprop="telephone">555-423-
2352</span>
<a href="http://googlemapsurl.com"
itemprop="maps">URL of Map</a>
</div>
```

For more detailed information on geographic markup and local SEO, I'd suggest taking a look at Search Engine Journal's article on how to use Schema markup for local SEO,[95] as well as Schema.org's Local Business section.[96]

Build backlinks that include location in anchor text

As we discussed in Chapter 7, backlinks are vital to the visibility of your site in search results. As you might expect, they're hugely important to local SEO too.

---

95 https://www.searchenginejournal.com/how-to-use-schema-markup-for-local-seo/60245/

96 http://schema.org/LocalBusiness

To boost performance in local search results, you should encourage anyone kind enough to give you a backlink to include the location of your business in the backlink. This emphasizes the location of your business to search engines.

To go back to our bike shop example, this would simply mean building links to 'bike shop Brixton' instead of 'bike shop.'

Create content which references your local area

As with much else in SEO, quality content can really help your cause. If you can write quality blog posts about your business niche which involve your local area, you may find yourself doing rather nicely in search results.

Using our bike shop example (again!), a way to get some traction in local search results might be to blog about good cycling routes in the area.

Try to get local coverage

It's definitely worth approaching local news sites asking for some coverage of your business (or content).

Given the local angle, many of these news sites will be more than happy to provide you with a backlink – and this backlink might pass on a significant amount of 'link juice.' News sites, even local ones, tend to have a lot of authority, because a lot of other sites link to them.

It's also likely that Google's algorithms will take note of the context in which these links appear – i.e., on sites which are about your local area – and associate your site with that location.

Chapter summary

Local SEO can often give you 'quick wins' in search results. This is because Google's focus on localized results means its algorithms often prioritize local, independent business over big brands.

Additionally, not all your local competitors will be aware of how local SEO works – this means you can often steal a march on them.

To maximize visibility in search results you should:

- Register your business with Google My Business.
- Include references to your location in all key parts of your site (title, headings, body copy, footer and URLs).
- Submit your site to local directories (note: quality ones only!).

- Encourage happy customers to review your site on Google My Business.

- Add geographic markup to your site.

- Build backlinks to your site which include your location in the anchor text.

- Create blog posts on your site which are specifically about your local area.

- Seek out coverage on local sites – this can generate some backlinks from authoritative sites to your domain, and may help Google associate your site with a particular area.

9 Social media and SEO

So far in this book we've looked at aspects of 'traditional' websites – publishing content on them, making technical changes to them or getting links from them to boost our position in search.

But obviously we are working in an online world which is dominated by social networks – with behemoths like Facebook, Twitter and Instagram dominating the digital landscape and generating huge traffic to websites.

But what is the relationship between social media and SEO? Well, to use a well-known social media phrase, it's complicated.

Is a 'like' or 'share' as valuable as a backlink?

You would be forgiven for thinking that Google treats every 'like' or share of a piece of content as a ranking signal. However, if the pronouncements from Google on this subject matter are to be believed, you would be wrong.[97]

And yet...content with lots of social media likes and shares does seem to end up at the top of search results. So, what's going on?

Well, the obvious thing to say (as Google do regarding this issue) is that correlation is not the same as causation.

---

97 https://www.youtube.com/watch?v=udqtSM-6QbQ

For example, a piece of great content that makes its way to the top of search results is more likely to be discovered by people who subsequently share it on social media. In other words, it's the search ranking that driving the social shares, not the other way round.

But things *can* work the other way round: a piece of content that goes viral on Facebook is likely to get seen by a lot of people, a proportion of whom then create links to it on non-social sites; this in turn can propel it to the top of search results.

In which case, you could argue that multiple shares of a piece of content on social media *does*, in fact, lead to higher search rankings.

The point is that the relationship is not 'direct' – a share of a piece of content is not a vote for it (in Google's eyes) and won't on its own affect your site's ranking.

But the relationship nonetheless exists and can lead to a nice little virtuous circle being created: a strong position in search results for a piece of content can lead to a lot of social shares of it, which can then result in people creating backlinks that reinforce that content's strong performance in search results. And so on.

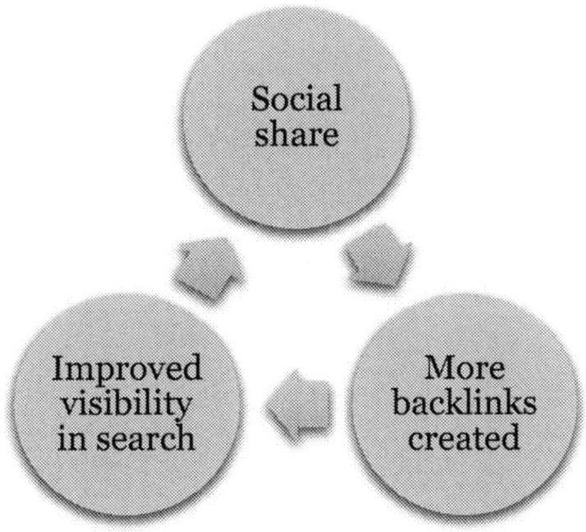

Social shares can lead to more backlinks being created – and vice versa...

Given all this, it's definitely worth investing time in maximizing the number of shares your content receives. The question is: how?

Maximizing the number of shares your content receives

1. Create shareworthy content

Yes, we're back here again, with our old friend 'quality content.' The content you publish on your site simply has to be so good that people will want to share it on social media. If your website pages and posts are 'inherently viral' the chances of them being shared extensively on social media are much greater.

2. Make your content very easy to share on social networks

You can make your content much easier to share simply by adding sharing buttons on your website. There are lots of services which allow you to add these, for example Sumo,[98] Addthis[99] and Sharethis.[100]

3. Actively encourage sharing

It's one thing having sharing buttons on your site – quite another getting people to use them. So always include a blindingly obvious 'please share' call to action on your site and any other material promoting your content (e-newsletters, Facebook posts etc.).

4. Consider using social ads

If you're confident that a piece of content you've created is genuinely wonderful and inherently viral, there is an argument to be made for promoting it using social ads (for example sponsored posts on Facebook or promoted tweets on Twitter).

This is a relatively cheap way to put the content in front of a niche audience who might be inclined either to share it further on social media, or create backlinks to it.

---

98 https://go.sumo.com/8396.html [note: this is an affiliate link]

99 http://www.addthis.com/

100 https://www.sharethis.com/

The value of social media profiles

So far in this chapter we've just talked about social shares and how these can impact on search results.

However, social media *profiles* (and their associated content – tweets, videos etc.) usually have a significant SEO value, because they frequently appear near the top of results for particular types of searches.

This is particularly true for searches for brand names:

- A Google search for U2 (and yes, they are a brand!) returns the band's Twitter page, latest tweets, Facebook page and Instagram page in the top ten results.

- Similarly, a search for John Lewis (a major UK high street retailer) returns their Twitter page and latest tweets just below the company's website.

When working on web design builds for clients, I usually find that until the SEO side of their project is fully completed, their Facebook or Twitter page often outranks their new website (or is much quicker to appear in search results than the actual site).

Given all this, it's clear that Google treats profiles from well-known social networks preferentially in search. This has a couple of implications for how you position yourself on social media.

First, you need to ensure your business has a presence on the major social networks. In the early days of your business, before Google has indexed your website fully and is displaying it in search results, having a Facebook page may be the difference between potential clients finding your business or not.

Second, you need to make sure that all your social media profiles are always bang up to date and that you check messages sent to them regularly.

Even if people searching for your business see your website occupying the number one spot for your brand name, they may prefer to click on a result for your Facebook page (so that they can get updates from you in that format).

When this happens your Facebook page, not your site, is their first impression of your business and as such you need to make sure it is a positive one.

Social networks as search engines

It's easy to forget that social networks are increasingly performing the role of search engine for millions of users. Think about it: all the major social networks have search boxes which can be used to locate profiles or content on those networks. And billions of users make queries on them every day.

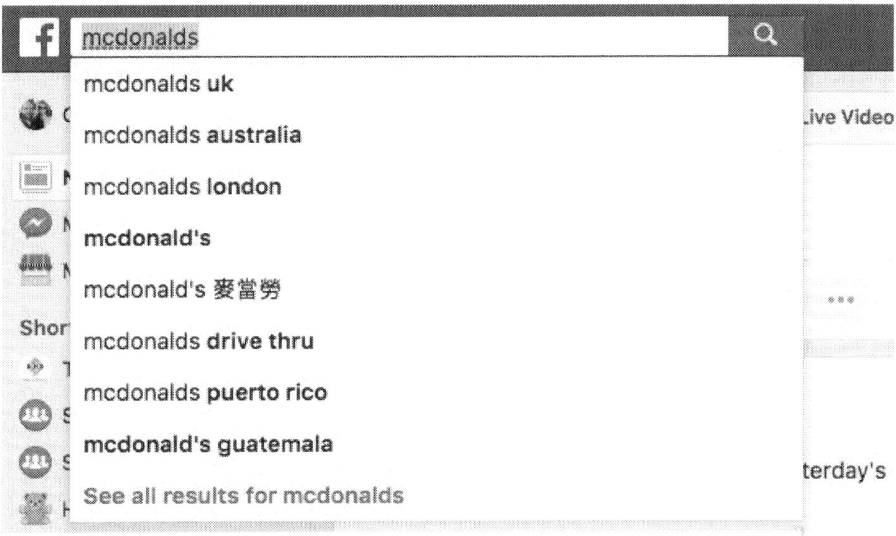

In Facebook, the search box is the first thing presented to the user, highlighting the fact that it's now not just a social network but a search engine too.

Accordingly, it's really important to:

- have profiles on these networks in the first place – without them, you are reducing the chances of your brand appearing in social search results

- ensure that you're optimizing your social media profiles so that they include keywords related to your business, along with accurate location information

- publish quality content on these networks which can show up in searches made on them.

This only scratches the surface of social SEO. For some excellent tips on how to take advantage of the search functionality on social networks, I'd suggest reading Neil Patel's article on the topic: Social SEO Simplified: How to Optimize for the "Other" Search Engines.[101]

Chapter summary

- Social shares can improve performance in search results – but in an indirect manner. A large number of social shares can increase the number of people viewing your content; a proportion of these visitors will then create backlinks to it on non-social sites, improving your search rankings in the process. It's important to note that it is the backlinks created via increased visibility of your content, rather than the actual social shares, that improve position in search results.

- You should aim to increase the number of shares of your content by publishing shareworthy content in the first

---

[101] https://www.quicksprout.com/2015/09/28/social-seo-simplified-how-to-optimize-for-the-other-search-engines/

place; adding sharing tools to your site; and actively encouraging your readers to share your content. If budget allows, you could also consider using social ads to increase the number of people reading (and sharing) your content on social media.

- Social profiles are given preferential treatment in search results, and therefore it is important to create profiles for your business on major social networks and keep them up to date.

- Don't overlook the fact that social networks are in fact search engines – this means that you should create profiles on the major networks and keep them up to date.

10 Using email marketing to improve search rankings

Throughout this book we've more or less divided SEO into three key areas:

- on-page SEO (all the things you can do to your content to improve its chances of appearing in search)
- off-page SEO (link building strategies)
- technical SEO (the technical tweaks you can make to your site to enhance its performance in search results).

However, there are other techniques you can use to boost your site's search ranking which don't neatly fit into these categories.

Using social media proactively, as I indicated in the previous chapter, is a classic example of such a technique. Although Google is on record as saying that its algorithms don't consider the number of social shares of your content when working out where to place your site in search results, these shares definitely increase the number of people eyeballing your content, which in turn increases the number of people who ultimately create a backlink to it.

Email marketing is another one of these 'peripheral' tactics which can be used to improve the performance of your site in search results, and in this chapter we're going to take a look at how you can use a mailing list and e-newsletters to influence the position of your content in search results.

The relationship between mailing list size and SEO

Just as Google doesn't take the size of your social media following into account when ranking your website in search, it is not going to take a look at the size of your mailing list (in fact it can't!) and conclude that because yours is bigger than your key competitor's, your site should be ranking higher in search.

However, size *does* matter, and here's why: the bigger your mailing list, the more people you can drive to your content via e-newsletters, and the more people you drive to your content, the greater the chance of some of them either

- creating a backlink to it (which has a direct impact on search results)
  or
- sharing it on social media (which can have an indirect impact on search results).

Furthermore, the people who went to the trouble of signing up to your mailing list are likely to be the most engaged consumers of your content – and by extension, the people who are most likely to create those valuable backlinks to it or share it on social networks.

The question is: how do you build a large mailing list?

How to grow a mailing list

The secret to mailing list growth usually lies in two things:

- Getting a *lot* of visitors to your website.
- Creating web pages that are optimized to convert these visitors to subscribers.

In terms of driving large quantities of traffic to your site, this is down to your SEO and/or online advertising efforts.

Only a small percentage of your website visitors will convert to email subscribers, and to maximize the number who do so, there are several tactics you should employ:

- **Ensure every page has a mailing list form prominently displayed on it**. For blog posts, you could even consider using two forms – one on the side, and one at the bottom of the post.

- **Spell out the benefits of subscribing to your mailing list extremely clearly above each sign up form**. Make it clear that your visitors will get extremely valuable content – like that which they've just read – if they sign up to your mailing list.

- **Include a 'subscribe' link** in your main navigation.

- **Use a squeeze page for any advertising campaigns you run**. If you're investing in online ads to grow your mailing list, it's usually best to use a dedicated landing page – a 'squeeze' page – rather than pointing users to one of your standard web pages. Squeeze pages can be designed to eliminate distraction (for example, they typically don't feature site navigation or social icons) and focus people on the task of completing an online form. You can also run A/B tests on squeeze pages, testing variants of them against each other, to make sure that you are using the highest converting landing page possible.

Example of a landing ('squeeze') page created with the Unbounce app. Note the absence of any site navigation or outbound links: the focus is completely on getting a user to complete a form.

Sending e-newsletters with SEO in mind

Once you're capturing subscribers onto your mailing list effectively, it's time to send e-newsletters to them in a way which actively improves your search results.

Directing people to your content

More often than not, business owners view e-newsletters as a way to sell stuff – to highlight special offers, new products and so on. This is all very well and good, but if you focus exclusively on using e-newsletters in this way, you are missing an SEO trick.

Whilst it's fine (and necessary) to send e-newsletters which promote your goods and services, if you're serious about improving your search rankings, you also need to focus on using e-newsletters to promote your *content* - the fantastic blog posts, infographics and free web tools that you have spent so long developing and publishing on your site.

Ideally, you should identify the really valuable content on your site and plan an email communications cycle which drives people to it.

The good news is that you can use automated emails called 'autoresponders' to manage this process for you.[102] Apps like Getresponse or Mailchimp allow you to set these up so that that every time somebody joins your mailing list they will automatically start receiving e-newsletters – at intervals of your choosing – which direct people to your content.[103]

---

102 https://www.stylefactoryproductions.com/blog/autoresponders

103 https://www.stylefactoryproductions.com/blog/getresponse-vs-mailchimp

You can go a step further with autoresponders by using 'marketing automation' to send particular pieces of content to the subscribers who are most likely to appreciate it.

For example, if you run a website about cars, you could use this automation to send articles about Audis to people who signed up in your Audi reviews section; articles about Toyotas to people who signed up in the Toyota section – and so on.

The effect of all this is to get more engaged people eyeballing your content – a key aim of all SEO work.

As I've said throughout the book, the more people consuming your content, the greater the chance of backlinks being created to it becomes; and more backlinks, as we know, means better search rankings.

Explicitly encouraging people to create backlinks

In Chapter 7 we looked at link-building tactics: an important one was outreach, where you contact people you don't know personally and ask them for a backlink to your site.

It's easy to forget that you can use your mailing list for this very same purpose. If you are in the fortunate position of having thousands of subscribers on your mailing lists, and a large number of quality posts on your site, why not encourage your most loyal followers to help you with your backlink building efforts?

In my e-newsletters to my subscribers, I come right out and say it:

Here's a link to a post you might find relevant to your business – if you enjoy it, it would be great if you could consider creating a link to it on your website or blog, or sharing it on social media.

Now, not everybody on your mailing list will have a website, but a proportion of your subscribers will, and even if only a small number of these site owners create a backlink to your site, this can have a highly beneficial impact on your search results.

Encouraging social sharing

It almost goes without saying at this point that it's a good idea to encourage people to share your newsletters – or the content they contain – on social media.

Most email marketing apps let you add social sharing icons to your newsletters easily enough, and some also allow you to connect your social profiles to the app so that your newsletters are automatically published on your social profiles as soon as they are broadcast.

And it doesn't hurt to include a 'please share on social media' text call-to-action in your e-newsletter either.

Chapter summary

- You can use email marketing to significantly increase the number of visitors to your website – this will increase the likelihood of backlinks to your site being created.

- The more email subscribers you have on your mailing list, the better this strategy will work.

- To increase the size of your mailing list, ensure you have mailing list sign-up forms placed prominently on your website, and consider using pop-up forms and welcome mats (judiciously) to convert visitors to subscribers.

- Spell out the benefits of joining the mailing list to your site visitors very clearly: there should be a definite quid-pro-quo for joining it.

- If running online advertising campaigns to capture leads, consider using squeeze pages to capture your visitors' details, as such pages tend to convert better than standard web pages.

- Ensure that you use your mailing list to promote not just your goods and services but your content too. You can use autoresponders to automate this process.

- In your email newsletters, you should explicitly ask people to create backlinks to the content you are sharing.

- Similarly, you should encourage social sharing of the articles featured in your e-newsletter.

11 Maintaining a site's performance in search results

By the end of a well-executed SEO project, your keyword research, fantastic content, on-page SEO, technical SEO and backlink building should all be yielding results and you should hopefully be enjoying good search results for your chosen keywords.

But things don't stop there – there are several things you need to do to ensure that once you're at the top of the search tree, you stay there.

Keep your content 'fresh'

Google has filed a number of patents on 'content freshness' over the years – these indicate that it treats pages and posts that are updated frequently preferentially to those that are not.[104]

Accordingly, there is a strong SEO argument for regularly updating your content so that it is always up to date.

Besides which, content which is up to date is more useful to your readers. If, for example, you review software on your blog, and your content consists of outdated analysis which neglects to mention the latest features of an application you're reviewing, the chance of

---

[104] https://moz.com/blog/google-fresh-factor-new

your readers sharing your content (either through backlink creation or social shares) diminishes significantly.

Some SEO experts believe that you should also add brand new content to your site fairly regularly – I would cautiously agree with this, but I'd emphasize that it is only ever worth putting new content on your website if it is genuinely valuable to your site visitors and that you have the time and resources available to promote it adequately and build backlinks to it once it's live. For me, content freshness is more about keeping good content *up to date* than constantly churning out new content.

Take care when changing URLs

In an ideal world, it's best not to change the URL of a page or post – especially one that is already performing well in search results.

There's a couple of reasons for this: first, SEO experts believe that there is always a degree of risk associated with moving a page from one location to another.[105]

Second, if you use social sharing tools to highlight how many shares there have been of that page / post, your counter will show zero after a URL change. This damages the 'social proof' of your page,

[105] https://moz.com/blog/301-redirection-rules-for-seo

making your content appear less 'authoritative' or popular than it did before you changed the URL it used to sit on.

That said, there are occasions when you simply do need to change URLs, and if you do so, you should always create a 'permanent' or '301' redirect to tell search engines where your page has moved to.[106]

There are various ways to do this – if you use a hosted website builder like Squarespace or Wix, you'll usually find a 'manage redirects' option which lets you create 301 redirects easily enough. If you're a WordPress user there are many plugins available to make the creation of 301 redirects straightforward.

If you are more technically-minded, you can also create redirects using a htaccess file[107] or use PHP to do so.[108]

Fix broken links

Broken links on your pages make for an annoying user experience and may discourage users from trusting, sharing and creating backlinks to your site.

---

106 https://support.google.com/webmasters/answer/93633?hl=en

107 http://www.htaccess-guide.com/redirects/

108 https://yoast.com/create-301-redirect-wordpress/

Additionally, there's reason to believe that Google's algorithms don't like to encounter them on your pages either; in its Google Search Console help resources,[109] the company explicitly advises webmasters to ensure that all links go to live web pages.

There are several tools available to help you find broken links on your site quickly – one of the best known is Screaming Frog.[110]

Not only should you fix broken links *from* your site, you should also fix broken links *to* your site. A broken link to your site is effectively a wasted backlink – Google generally won't count it as a 'vote' for your content if it's taking the user to a 404 'not found' page.

Usually you'll find broken links to your site appearing after you've changed a page's URL without creating a redirect.

Most of the main keyword research tools allow you to see a list of broken links to your website – you can use this list to identify problem URLs and create redirects for them (thus ensuring you're not missing out on any valuable backlinks).

---

109 https://support.google.com/webmasters/answer/35769?hl=en#1

110 https://www.screamingfrog.co.uk/broken-link-checker/

Get rid of low-quality links to your site

Google is opaque about many issues relating to its search algorithm, but one thing it is crystal clear on is the fact that it hates spammy or low-quality links.

Here's what they have to say about them:

> Google works very hard to make sure that actions on third-party sites do not negatively affect a website. In some circumstances, incoming links can affect Google's opinion of a page or site. For example, you or a search engine optimizer (SEO) you've hired may have built bad links to your site via paid links or other link schemes that violate our quality guidelines...We recommend that you remove as many spammy or low-quality links from the web as possible.[111]

There are two ways you'll end up with spammy links:

- You were naughty and created a bunch of them on low-quality, irrelevant websites (or hired somebody to do so).
- One of your competitors has engaged in 'negative SEO' and deliberately created a ton of spammy links to your site.[112]

---

[111] https://support.google.com/webmasters/answer/2648487?hl=en

[112] https://searchengineland.com/6-types-negative-seo-watch-272881

To identify potentially 'toxic' links, you can either:

- download all your backlinks in Google Search Console (Dashboard > Links > Export External Links > Export Latest Links), and review each one to see if it's spammy – be careful though as some spammy links may take you through to dubious sites (containing explicit content or encouragements to download spyware etc.)

  or

- use a keyword search tool that allows you to identify suspicious links (Semrush is good for this).[113]

If you find yourself in a situation where you notice that you have a lot of low-quality backlinks pointing to your website, it is important to try to get rid of them, because the chances are that they will lead to a penalty from Google (this is discussed in more depth below – see the 'Penalties and how to deal with them' section).

The best option is to try to get them removed entirely from the web, by contacting the owner of the website providing the link in question and asking them to remove the link.

---

113 https://www.semrush.com/

However, this is not always possible – contact details may not be available or you may be dealing with shady webmasters (or no webmaster at all if you're dealing with sites that generate content automatically).

In this situation, you need to 'disavow' the link using a tool provided by Google in its Search Console. This tells Google not to consider it a backlink to your website when evaluating where it should sit in search results.

However, you need to be *extremely* careful when using this tool, as disavowing the wrong sort of links can result in a big dip in your site's search ranking. Before you disavow a link, you need to be 100% certain that it's definitely a 'toxic' one.

To disavow links you need to:

1. Identify 'toxic' links as described using the process above.

2. Compile a text file containing a list of these links, in the format requested by Google.[114]

3. Upload this file to Google using its disavow tool.[115]

---

114 https://support.google.com/webmasters/answer/2648487?hl=en

115 https://www.google.com/webmasters/tools/disavow-links-main

Google gives rather conflicting advice regarding when to use the disavow tool.

In their official help page on the tool, Google says:

> We recommend that you disavow backlinks only if you believe you have a considerable number of spammy, artificial, or low-quality links pointing to your site, and if you are *confident that the links are causing issues for you* [emphasis mine]. [116]

But in a video on this topic on the Google Webmasters Channel, Matt Cutts says this:

> If you're *at all worried* [emphasis mine] about somebody trying to do negative SEO, or it looks like there's some weird bot that's building up a bunch of links to your site, and you have no idea where it [sic] came from, that's a perfect time to use disavow as well.[117]

Which advice you decide to follow is unfortunately up to you (!) – but my general approach is that if I spot a link that is *unquestionably* toxic, and I can't get rid of it by contacting the person who created it, I add it to a disavow file.

---

[116] https://support.google.com/webmasters/answer/2648487?hl=en

[117] https://www.youtube.com/watch?v=eFJZXpnsRsc

One thing that's important to note with regard to a disavow file is that it should be a 'rolling' file – i.e., you should add toxic links to the existing set and re-upload *all* of them every time you use the disavow tool. Otherwise Google will only disavow the links in your *latest* version of your disavow file.

I would strongly encourage you to read Google's support material on the disavow tool before using it.[118] Ahref's guide to link quality[119] also contains a lot of information on toxic links and how to identify and disavow them.

Follow Search Console's advice

Earlier I discussed how you can use Search Console to tell Google important things about your site – for example, where it is on the web, what pages it contains and the location of the users you are hoping to target with your content.

However, Search Console also provides an opportunity for Google to tell *you* things about your site; you can use the tool to get a list of things you need to improve or fix to ensure continued good placement for your site in search results.

---

[118] https://support.google.com/webmasters/answer/2648487?hl=en

[119] https://ahrefs.com/blog/bad-links/

The areas in Search Console which I'd suggest you keep a close eye on and check regularly are as follows:

Search performance

As its name suggests, the 'performance' report in Google Search Console allows you to get a good sense of how your content is performing in its search results.[120]

It allows you to check on the number of impressions it receives when people search for it; the number of clicks through to it; and its average position in search results. You can use all this data to make improvements to specific pieces of content so that they perform better in search results.

The main way to do this is to look at the search queries which are generating a lot of impressions for your content, but *not* click-throughs. You can then use this information to make changes to underperforming pages, so that their page titles and meta descriptions become more engaging (and more likely to be clicked on). You can then use the performance report to monitor the effect of these modifications on your click-through rate over time.

You can also use this report to help you 'nudge' certain pieces of content up the search ranking. For example, if one your site's pages

---

[120] https://support.google.com/webmasters/answer/7576553

is averaging at around the number 5 spot in search results, it might only take a couple more backlinks to get it up to number one (something that will lead to a *lot* more click-throughs to your site). The performance report lets you spot these 'quick wins' very easily and helps you target your backlink outreach accordingly.

And finally, you can use this report to help you identify if you've been at the end of an algorithmic penalty from Google (more on which below).

URL Inspection

The URL inspection tool in Search Console allows you to look at an individual URL to see

- if it has been indexed successfully by Google
- if there are any technical issues with the URL that are preventing it from appearing in search results (and if so, what these issues are).

A useful application of the URL inspection tool is for submitting new content to Google for indexing (for example, a new page or post on your site that Google has not discovered through crawling yet). When you do this, it is added to a 'priority crawl' queue which may result in this content appearing more quickly in search results.

Similarly, you can use this tool to *re-index* existing content — if you have just updated a page and would like Google to take note of the changes more quickly, you can use the URL inspection tool to do this too.

Coverage report

The 'coverage' section of Search Console allows you to see what sections of your website Google cannot index — you can click on the 'Excluded' tab in this report to see a list of pages from your website that are not in Google's index.[121]

Most of the time the stuff you'll see in this area of Search Console involves sections of your site that you won't particularly want indexed, but it's worth keeping an eye on periodically, just in case anything that you *do* want to see in search results slips in there.

Mobile usability

As Google puts it, 'websites with mobile usability issues may not rank as well in mobile search results'. You can find out whether Google thinks your site has these sort of issues (and what you should do to fix them) in Search Console by using its mobile usability report.[122]

---

[121] https://support.google.com/webmasters/answer/7440203

[122] https://support.google.com/webmasters/answer/9063469

Accelerated Mobile Pages (AMP)

If you use Accelerated Mobile Pages (AMP) to create faster-loading versions of your mobile pages (which, as discussed in Chapter 6, is a very good idea), then you can use Search Console's Accelerated Mobile Pages report to see if there are any problems with how you've constructed them, along with recommended fixes for any problem.[123]

Manual actions

If you spot something in Search Console's 'manual actions' report, you're in trouble![124] This means that a real human being from Google has noticed that you've been creating dodgy links to your site (or using other underhand methods to boost your site's position in search) and has applied a 'manual action penalty' to your site.

The consequences of this are significant – but there are ways to get out of this hole (see the 'Penalties and how to deal with them' section below).

---

123 https://support.google.com/webmasters/answer/7450883

124 https://support.google.com/webmasters/answer/9044175

Security Issues

As you might expect, the 'security issues' section of Search Console tells you if your site has any security problems – for example, if it's been hacked.[125]

Links to your site

The 'links' section in Search Console is useful for a couple of reasons.

First, it lets you get a general sense of how successful your link building efforts are. If you're just finding tumbleweed in this section, or you notice a marked slow-down on the number of external links to your site being created, it's time to get more proactive with your link-building activities.

The 'links to your site' section also allows you to spot any spammy links and disavow them where necessary (see the 'Getting rid of low-quality links to your site' section above for more detail).

Penalties and how to deal with them

As I've mentioned quite a few times in this book already, Google's algorithms *hate* spammy practices – paid-for links, link schemes

---

125 https://support.google.com/webmasters/topic/4598273?visit_id=636860953932861896-497971175

and so on – and site owners that use these tactics to improve their site's position in search can and do get penalized for doing so.

There are two types of Google penalty:

- An **'algorithmic' penalty**, which can be applied if Google's algorithms are not satisfied by the quality of your content or backlinks.
- A **'manual action' penalty**, which is applied after a human being (!) looks at your site, its content and its backlinks and concludes that something very fishy is going on.

Having either type of penalty applied to your site can have very serious consequences for your business, but fortunately – with a bit of work – it is possible to get both removed.

How to spot a penalty

The first sign that your site has been penalized — either manually or algorithmically — is a sharp drop in organic traffic (which you can easily spot by using Google Analytics and/or the performance report in Search Console).

To find out whether this is due to an algorithmic penalty or a manual action penalty, you need to check the manual actions report in Google Search Console.[126]

If you have a manual action penalty to deal with, you will be notified here; if not, you are probably dealing with an algorithmic penalty.

Recovering from an algorithmic penalty

Although the phrase 'algorithmic penalty' is frequently used by SEO experts, Google engineer Matt Cutts has suggested in the past that the phrase may actually be something of a misnomer.[127]

Cutts points out that if you notice a sharp drop in traffic, it's not necessarily Google *penalizing* you for bad behaviour. For example,

- one of your competitors might have created some content on your niche topic that is considerably better than yours and is now outranking it
- you may have lost some valuable backlinks recently
- you may have erroneously asked Google not to index a particular page in a robots.txt file.[128]

---

[126] https://support.google.com/webmasters/answer/9044175

[127] https://www.youtube.com/watch?v=6voLG6FHzTE

[128] https://moz.com/learn/seo/robotstxt

In other words, a *penalty* is not necessarily being applied; it may be more a case of changes to your site (or to others) resulting in Google's algorithm treating your content less favourably.

If you believe one of the above scenarios to be the cause of a sudden dip in traffic, then addressing the issue is fairly straightforward – you essentially need to improve your content, link building and technical SEO work using the methods described earlier in this book.

However, if you see a significant rise in the number of spammy links to your site at the same time as a big dip in the organic traffic to your site, it is possible to conclude that to all intents and purposes Google's algorithms *are* indeed penalizing you.

If this is the case, you may need to take some additional action: removing the offending links to your website or disavowing them in Search Console when removal is not possible (see 'Getting rid of low-quality links to your site' above for instructions on how to do this).

The bottom line when it comes to overcoming algorithmic penalties is that a combination of improved SEO practices alongside removal / disavowal of low-quality links usually solves the problem.

Recovering from a manual action penalty

Manual action penalties can have a profoundly negative effect on your search traffic, and by extension your business.

You will usually have been at the receiving end of a Google manual action penalty if you have aggressively and knowingly engaged in activities that violate Google's quality guidelines, namely using the below techniques to boost your site's performance in search:[129]

- Automatically generating content
- Participating in link schemes
- Creating pages with little or no original content
- Cloaking
- Using sneaky redirects
- Creating hidden text or links
- Using doorway pages
- Scraping content from other sites
- Participating in affiliate programmes without adding sufficient value
- Loading pages with irrelevant keywords
- Creating pages with malicious behaviour, such as phishing or installing viruses, trojans, or other badware
- Abusing rich snippets markup

---

129 https://support.google.com/webmasters/topic/6001971?hl=en&ref_topic=6001981

- Sending automated queries to Google.

The good news is that

- you *can* recover from manual penalties
- not all of your site will necessarily be affected if you receive a manual penalty – Google may just take action against some of the pages on it
- Google is quite explicit in its manual actions report regarding what has led to you receiving the manual action penalty in the first place.

To address a manual action penalty, you'll need to look at the manual actions report in Search Console, examine the reason why you've been penalized and put a halt to the spammy practice that has led to the penalty being applied in the first place.

This may involve spending quite a lot of time on link removal and/or disavowal.

Once you're satisfied that you've done everything you can to meet Google's requirements, you can request reconsideration of your site.[130]

---

130 https://www.google.com/webmasters/tools/reconsideration

It can take a while for Google to respond to this request – based on my reading around the topic, it can take several weeks for Google to reply and/or remove the penalty.

All the more reason to avoid getting one in the first place!

Chapter summary

Maintaining a good position in search results requires ongoing work. The key things you should do to maintain one are listed below.

- Keep your content up to date.

- Avoid changing your site domain URL and the URLs of pages and posts), if at all possible.

- If you *do* need to change a page's URL, make sure you've created a '301 redirect' to it.

- Fix all broken links to and from your website. Tools such as Screaming Frog can help you with this.

- Get rid of any spammy links to your site (or disavow them when this is not possible). Be very careful during the disavow process however – make sure it is 100% necessary and only disavow links that you are absolutely certain are toxic in nature and actively damaging your website's search rankings.

- Use Search Console along with Google Analytics regularly to monitor the health of your website and deal with any algorithmic or manual penalties that may have been applied to it.

12 Summary / further reading and resources

I hope you've found this book to be a useful introduction to the world of search engine optimization.

Although some aspects of SEO can be complicated, for me things always boil down to the three golden rules that I outlined at the start of book:

1. Find out what people are searching for in your business area.
2. Create really good content on your site.
3. Get links from quality sites to that content.

It is important to remember however, that optimizing your site for search engines is not a one-off event: over time, your competition will change; Google's algorithms will change; and the products or services that you are writing about will change.

As such you should view SEO as a *process* - something that you invest time in on an ongoing basis; and it's very important to keep abreast of the latest developments in the field.

To this end I would suggest bookmarking the websites below, which will help you stay up to date with the latest thinking on SEO as well as news about important changes to Google algorithms.

- Google's Webmaster Central blog[131]
- The Moz blog[132]
- SEO blog by Ahrefs[133]
- Search Engine Journal[134]
- Search Engine Land[135]
- Backlinko blog[136]

I would also encourage you to sign up to the Style Factory mailing list, if you have not done so already – I regularly share SEO tips via Style Factory's e-newsletter.[137]

Finally, overleaf you will find a series of 'cheat sheets' to help you quickly perform the key SEO tasks outlined in this book. These are checklists which you can run through every time you create a new website or piece of content.

Good luck with making Google love your website!

---

131 https://webmasters.googleblog.com/

132 https://moz.com/blog

133 https://ahrefs.com/blog/

134 https://www.searchenginejournal.com/

135 https://searchengineland.com/

136 https://backlinko.com/blog

137 https://www.stylefactoryproductions.com/subscription/

13 Cheat sheets

The below 'cheat sheets' are checklists of the key tasks you'll need to complete when optimizing a piece of content (or indeed an entire website) for Google. Print them out and use them as a guide when working on an SEO project.

Writing quality content

Task	Examples / notes	☑
Choose the right format for your content	This will vary by business type but in most cases, blog posts generate the most 'indexable,' Google-friendly content.	☐
Ensure that the person creating your blog posts is a great writer	He or she should have an extensive knowledge of your business area along with great writing skills.	☐
Write posts that address known search queries	Perform keyword research to identify topics that people are interested in.	☐
Write posts that solve problems	Use 'how to' posts and listicles to create shareworthy, 'actionable' content.	☐
Be original	Never 'scrape' or duplicate other people's content.	☐

Ensure that your content's title is as engaging as possible, and relevant to the queries you are trying to address	Good titles lead to higher clickthrough rates, which can improve search rankings.	☐
Create great opening paragraphs that make it clear how you are going to solve the reader's key problem	Good, relevant opening paragraphs keep the reader on the page longer, leading to a longer 'dwell time' which may improve a page's position in search results.	☐
Ensure that your content is 'long-form'	Write in-depth articles that have a high word- count (> 1,000 words). These typically perform better in search results.	☐
Create engaging content that keeps your visitor on the page for as long as possible	Use images, infographics and videos to keep your visitor engaged with your content for as long as possible (again, with the aim of increasing 'dwell time').	☐
Ensure your content is very easy to read	Use san-serif typefaces to present your text (and sub-headings, short paragraphs and bullet points to break it up clearly).	☐

On-page SEO

Task	Examples / notes	☑
Use simple, clean URLs for your pages, and ensure that they include your target keywords	Example: www.mysite.com/green-dresses instead of www.mysite.com/gd#2017	☐
Start your page titles with your keywords	Example: Green dresses from Jill's Dress Shop.	☐
Expand your page titles with helpful 'long-tail' keywords	Example: Green dresses from Jill's Vintage Dress Shop in Brixton, London.	☐
Include your target keywords in H1 tags		☐
Ensure your page titles and H1 tags are unique	This helps you avoid any 'duplicate content' problems, which Google is not a fan of.	☐
Write compelling meta descriptions (135-160 characters) that include your focus keyword	Example: Our wide range of beautiful vintage green dresses can help you create a stunning 1970s look. Go retro at Jill's Vintage Dress Shop in Brixton, London.	☐
Include your target keyword in the first paragraph of your page content		☐

Include target keywords in some H2s		☐
Include your target keywords a few times in your copy		☐
Make sure your content is fairly long	Ideally, your posts should contain over 1,000 words.	☐
Increase dwell time by including useful videos, images or infographics on your page		☐
Add LSI (Latent Semantic Index) keywords to your content	In an article with a focus keyword of 'retro dresses', this might mean including references to 'vintage outfits' or '70s attire' as well as 'retro dresses.'	☐
Add 'alt text' to your images which includes your focus keywords	Note that this should not just be for SEO purposes but for accessibility reasons too.	☐
Add outbound links from your pages to relevant, authoritative websites	For example, in a post on fashion, you could include links to the *Vogue* or *Elle* websites.	☐
Encourage social sharing of your content	This can be done through calls-to-action and the addition of social sharing icons.	☐

Encourage visitors to comment on your posts	Issue a clear 'please comment on this article' call-to-action at the end of your posts.	☐
Add rich snippets to your content	Rich snippets (star ratings, pricing info etc.) can help content stick out in search results and generate higher clickthrough rates.	☐

Technical SEO

Task	Examples / notes	☑
Use SSL on your website if at all possible	Google treats secure websites preferentially in search results, but be careful when moving from http:// to https:// as getting this wrong can have negative SEO consequences.	☐
Ensure you use a responsive website that performs well on mobile	A responsive website is one that resizes your site automatically to suit all device types.	☐
Use the fastest hosting provider you can		☐
Use the fastest DNS provider you can		☐
Avoid use of interstitials, particularly on mobile devices	Interstitials are large pop-ups and banners that get in the way of your content.	☐
Don't use Flash	Use HTML 5 if you need to add special effects to your web pages.	☐

Use AMP (Accelerated Mobile Pages) format where possible.	This is a stripped-down format of your content which loads faster on mobile devices.	☐
Keep HTTPs requests to a minimum	This means removing non-essential scripts and content from the pages on your site.	☐
Use one CSS stylesheet to cater for your website's design	This helps your site load faster, and site speed is a ranking signal.	☐
Enable compression on your website.	This generally involves using a file format / software called GZIP.	☐
Minify your site's code	This removes unnecessary code from your site and helps it load faster.	☐
Optimize all your images via cropping and compression before uploading them.	Image file sizes should be as small as possible, but avoid using pixelated pictures.	☐
Fix any duplicate content issues.	If duplicate content is absolutely necessary, use the 'rel=canonical' attribute to tell Google where the preferred version is located.	☐
Create and verify a property in Google's Search Console for each version of your site.	Create properties for all versions of your site (www, non-www, http:// and https://).	☐
Create an XML sitemap for your website		☐

Submit your XML sitemap to Search Console		☐
Use Search Console's 'Target Country' option to set your audience's location	Setting a target country will mean that your site may be treated preferentially in your own country	☐
Add Google Analytics to your site.	This will help you spot improvements you can make to your site to improve search rankings.	☐

Backlink building

Task	Examples / notes	☑
Create long, quality content!	Quality in-depth posts can generate lots of the 'natural links' that Google loves, simply as a result of its inherently viral nature.	☐
Perform email outreach	Ask both personal contacts and site owners that you don't know to create backlinks to your content.	☐
Guest post (carefully!)	Post only on quality site; don't over-optimize the anchor text in the backlinks you create in your guest posts; and limit the number of backlinks you include in your posts.	☐
Use a PR agency or press release distribution service to launch new products or services	Press release distribution can generate a high number of backlinks quickly – but make sure you are using a	☐

	reputable service or agency to handle this.	
Use broken link building to identify backlink opportunities	This involves finding links to content that don't work anymore, and trying to get the site owners to replace these with links to your content.	☐
Provide useful, free web tools	Examples include free privacy policies; tax calculators; currency convertors etc. If these perform useful tasks, site owners will often link to the pages where they can be downloaded.	☐
Use web alerts to find sites publishing new content related to your business area – and ask the owners of these for a backlink	You can use free tools like Google Alerts, or paid-for ones such as Ahrefs, for this purpose.	☐
Run surveys and publish the results	This gives you an opportunity to ask webmasters to feature a link to both the survey and the results on their sites.	☐
Consider using online advertising to boost the visibility of your content	This can help you generate some backlinks to new content. Facebook advertising is particularly useful in this regard – many companies routinely use Facebook ads to publicise blog posts.	☐
Issue a clear call-to-action on your blog posts to encourage readers to create a backlink to it.		☐

Local SEO

Task	Examples / notes	☑
Register your business with Google My Business	This will ensure that your site appears on map results – and as these appear above text-based search results, this can help you leap-frog competitors who have not registered with Google My Business.	☐
Include references to your location in all key parts of your site	This should include title, headings, body copy, footer and URLs.	☐
Submit your site to local directories	These should only include high-quality directories (ideally ones that vet submissions).	☐
Encourage happy customers to review your site on Google My Business	This can help improve clickthrough rate.	☐
Add Schema's geographic markup to your site		☐
Build backlinks to your site which include your location in the anchor text		☐
Create blog posts on your site which are specifically about your local area		☐

Seek out coverage on local news sites	This can generate some backlinks from authoritative sites to your domain, and may help Google associate your site with a particular area.	☐

Maintaining a good position in search results

Task	Examples / notes	☑
Keep your content up to date	Google's patents on 'content freshness' indicate that it's advisable to ensure that any articles or reviews on your site are refreshed regularly to ensure that they are up to date.	☐
Avoid changing your site domain URL (and the URLs of pages and posts)	Changing a URL can reduce the value of any existing backlinks you have to it, and damage the 'social proof' of a page by resetting its social media share counters to zero. (This is more of an issue with domains or pages that have been live for a long period of time).	☐
If you do need to change a URL, make sure you've created a '301 redirect' to it	A 301 redirect tells Google where the new content now resides and will preserve *most* of the value of any backlinks pointing to it.	☐
Identify and fix all broken links to and from your website	Tools like Screaming Frog can help with this.	☐
Identify and remove spammy links to your site, or	Be very careful during the disavow process however – make sure it is 100% necessary and only disavow links that you are absolutely certain are toxic in nature and actively damaging your website's search rankings.	☐

disavow them when this is not possible		
Use Search Console along with Google Analytics regularly to monitor the health of your website	This will help you to identify any algorithmic or manual penalties that may have been applied to it, and take the necessary steps to remove them.	☐

Acknowledgements

I would like to thank my father, David Singleton, for casting an editorial eye over this book; huge thanks also to my wife Emma Finnigan for her support during the writing and promotion of it.

Gratitude must also be expressed to my good friend Diarmaid Mac Mathúna, who read at least half of the book and gave some valuable feedback regarding the first 6 chapters.

If things go downhill after that, you can take it up with Diarmaid ☺

Printed in Great Britain
by Amazon

35285746R00109